Crown of Fire

Polycarp
Bishop of Smyrna

D1715621

Crown of Fire

Polycarp
Bishop of Smyrna

William Chad Newsom

CHRISTIAN FOCUS

Published by Christian Focus Publications, Geanies House, Fearn, Tain,
Ross-shire, IV20 1TW, Scotland, United Kingdom.
www.christianfocus.com email: info@christianfocus.com
Cover design by Alister Macinnes Cover illustration by Fred Apps
Printed and bound in Denmark by Nørhaven Paperback A/S

> We love the martyrs, but the Son of God we
> worship: it is impossible for us to worship any other.
> Eusebius of Caesarea

Acknowledgments

The list of those people to whom I owe much is far too long to be included here,
to my regret. I do wish to thank my friends at Christian Focus Publications for
giving me the opportunity and for believing in this work. To everyone in my
family— for encouragement, love, and support of every kind—I must attempt a
tale of gratitude that words can only begin to tell. This book does begin that tale,
I hope, if it reflects some of the goodness, truth, and beauty I have known among
you all. Especially, though, I wish to thank my Father and Mother, William and
Patsy Newsom. Dad taught me to love good books, and Mom taught me to love
good words. She also, along with my wife, patiently read the entire manuscript
and offered many valuable suggestions. To all of you, my thanks and love.

Dedication

To my wife Angela, and my children, Grace and William. This book is an emblem
of the storytelling culture we are building together in our home. May God bless
us as we tell the great tales—when we sit in our house, when we walk by the
way, when we lie down, and when we rise up. I love you with all my heart. And to
Polycarp, Papias, Ignatius, and Irenaeus: studying the lives and writings of these
great men has been an honor and a joy. I hope I have done some justice, at least,
to their remarkable story.

Contents

The Bishop of Lyons

Lyons, Gaul, Anno Domini, 177

"There!" shouted Severus to his companions. "Not far ahead—I see them!" He was one of about thirty, mostly men, who had been roaming the streets of Lyons for nearly an hour. The rain, twisted and swirled by the powerful winds, flew in their faces, nearly blinding them.

"How can you tell?" cried one of the others. "I can see someone up ahead, but I'm not certain——"

"It's them all right," replied Severus. "Why else would anyone be out on a night like this?"

"You're right, Severus," said the other. "On the way to one of their secret meetings, I'll wager."

"That's it," said Severus. "Besides, I saw the one of their faces when he turned back for a moment. It was him that tried to get my daughter to join their foul company. Oh, I'll never forget that face. Filthy little——"

"Never mind that now," said a third man. "We'd best hurry, before they get away."

Severus saw the sense in this and he and the others resumed the hunt. They had been waiting for this night for weeks now, ever since the new laws had been passed. And now they had finally found them, caught them in the act, or nearly, anyway. These are criminals we are hunting, plain and simple, thought Severus to himself. It's a good thing we're doing: good for the City and the Empire.

The "criminals" entered a narrow alley and kept going, their silent pursuers moving cautiously some way behind. Within a few minutes, the alley opened onto a wide lane— the main street of Lyons, with beautiful stone buildings lining either side. They stopped, as if unsure of the way. Severus smiled, and prepared to narrow the gap, but before he could do so, a sound reached his ears, and he halted his band of hunters. Three Roman soldiers were walking by on the road beyond the alley, hunched over in the rain. Though convinced that those he pursued were outlaws, Severus seemed just as dismayed as they were at the sight of official guardsmen of the law.

But the soldiers, hurrying through the downpour, did not see either group of people. The first group turned left down the street and Severus prepared to lead his company back into the hunt.

"Wait—Severus, just a moment," said one of the men.

Severus turned back, irritated at the delay. "What is it? Be quick."

"I—" the man looked warily around him at the wet, dark streets. "Maybe this is not a good idea."

"What in the name of all the gods are you talking about?"

"The soldiers," said the man, "there may be more of them. And what if these people aren't as timid as you say they are? Several of them were young and strong. We may have a fight on our hands. I'm afraid that—"

"You're what?" Severus nearly shouted the words, his teeth clenched and his eyes narrowed in a barely suppressed rage.

The man looked around again, tension evident in his rain-streaked face. "I said I'm afraid. Maybe we should—"

But he never finished his sentence. Severus suddenly lashed out, bringing his fist crashing onto the man's jaw. Then he grabbed the stunned man, dragged him back through the crowd, and flung him into the alley.

Severus cursed vilely at the man as he crawled away. Then he turned back to his companions. "He's a coward, just like them. That's why I hate them." He turned down the street, back into the hunt, muttering to himself. "That's why I hate them." His companions followed him, quickening their pace to make up for lost time.

Their urgency had the desired effect: only minutes later, they caught up at last, and surrounded their quarry. The little group of people, encircled by their enemies, stood still, awaiting the next move. A tense silence greeted them, broken only by the rain on the pavement, the heavy breathing of Severus and his friends, and a blast of thunder in the distance. At last, one of the captives spoke.

"Good evening, friends. What business have you with us?" The voice was steady and calm. The speaker—the young man Severus had spotted earlier—looked into the eyes of his hunters, and met the hateful gaze of Severus. Severus was tall, middle-aged, and strongly built. There was a black cloth patch where his right eye should have been, the result of a tavern brawl many years earlier. The young man had dark hair, and blue eyes, and with a sinking heart he recognized Severus, remembering the poisonous threats the older man had hurled at him when last they had met.

There was no response to the young man's question, but Severus and his friends began to glance at one another. Cruel smiles began to form on each face, and several began to laugh out loud. Soon the whole mob was shaking with vicious, gleeful laughter.

"Here's our business!" shouted one of the few women in the crowd. She picked up a rock from the street and threw it with all her might at the young man. It struck him on the arm, but he did not cry out or flinch. Others in Severus' crowd began throwing small stones, sticks, and other handy missiles (many brought along for just this purpose) at the young man and his friends. Others were content merely to laugh and taunt.

Severus picked up a stone, and shoved his way through the crowd to get a better angle. The captives—perhaps ten or twelve at the most—could not run, for the violent horde had surrounded them. Severus prepared to take aim at the hated young man, but at that moment his target spoke up. For a moment at least, the angry crowd halted their deadly pastime and listened.

"Please! Fellow citizens of Lyons! We mean you no harm. We know the law has forbidden us to visit public places. We are on our way to a private home to gather and worship our God. We pray only for the good of this city and of its people. We obey the laws, and seek to be honest, useful citizens. Why then do you hate us? For what crime do you torment us? What have we——"?

"Go back to Jewry, atheist!" Severus hurled his stone at the speaker. It struck him on the side of the head. Blood shot forth and the young man fell to the ground. The terrible act of violence only maddened the frenzied rabble. They pressed in on their prey——these helpless victims, now trying to help their fallen friend. More stones were thrown, and two more fell to the ground. Shouts and curses were hurled at the little band, and some were trying to drag them out of the crowd, the better to beat them properly. Blood lust ran through the mob like fire through a barn, and it looked as if nothing would save the unfortunate lambs from their wolfish wrath.

As the confusion developed into a near riot, the sound of heavy marching was suddenly heard on the street, and a small contingent of soldiers pushed its way through the throng of people. A shock of lightning lit the black sky, revealing the stern countenances and bright armor of the heavily armed Roman warriors. The wind whipped their red cloaks about them——in the gloom, the storm-tossed night, they appeared as gods to the pagan men of Lyons.

"Hold——what's all this?" The words came from a tall soldier, obviously the leader. The other soldiers held back the crowd, and the centurion knelt beside the bewildered victims, still trying to shelter their wounded.

The centurion looked up at the wild mass of people surrounding him. There was a glint of anger in his eyes, and a hint of sarcasm in his voice as he spoke. "Tell me, good citizens of Lyons," he said. "What crime have these people done to deserve stoning?" No one answered. A young woman, cradling the bloody and unconscious head of the man Severus had hit——her brother, in fact——spoke up through her tears, and her face, though bearing a look of suffering, showed a quiet determination. There was an air about her that those around could only interpret as peace, though of a kind they could not understand.

"We have committed no crime." Her voice was quiet, but unwavering. "We seek only to worship our God in peace—to observe our faith as He has taught us. And for this we are hunted and attacked. We are not rebels or revolutionaries. We seek not the overthrow of the Empire, nor do we hold her Law in contempt."

"They are Christians!" shouted Severus. "Their very existence is contempt for Rome's Law!" The mob roared its approval.

"Quiet!" demanded the centurion. "Go home! All of you—this is no concern of yours. Away! And that means you too, Severus. I might have known you were in the middle of this." The crowd sulked and grumbled—their fun had been cut too short—but under the threat of the soldiers' swords, they disbanded and went their separate ways, returning to their homes for sleep, and whatever brutal dreams such men have. But Severus hid in the shadows nearby, to see what would become of the hated Christians.

The centurion spoke to the girl in a kindly voice. "Tell me, lady: are you Roman citizens?"

"Several of us are. But my brothers and I are not."

A frown of concern crossed the centurion's face. "Then I must take you to the Governor. I...I truly wish there were some other way. The Governor, I fear, will prove no friend to you Christians. Nor will he feel compelled to any sense of justice when dealing with non-citizens."

The girl smiled weakly in gratitude. "Thank you," she said. "But God is King. He will protect us, if it is His will."

"And if He does not?"

She closed her eyes. It was a question she had often pondered. On the pages of her imagination, she seemed to see a hand, ageless and strong, writing names in the book of her memory— John the Baptist, James, Peter, Paul, Ignatius, Polycarp—names that gave her just enough courage and hope to speak.

"Then we shall gladly join with those who have borne witness to the grace of Christ by laying down their lives."

11

The centurion looked in her eyes with wonder at such a measure of courage in one so young. "You obviously understand the severity of the situation. You would give up everything, to die for this Christ?"

"Yes." She looked at him with unwavering eyes, sensing that she was in the middle of a Story, the plot of which had brought her and the soldier to this moment and these words. "All things I count loss already for Him who is everything to me."

The soldier, visibly moved, glanced down at her brother, still unconscious. "We must be quick," he said, pushing down the emotions rising in him. "He needs a doctor right away."

He picked up the fallen young man, who moaned in pain, breathing out incoherent words. Glancing around, the centurion saw ten others besides the girl and her brother. Some were about the same age, and several were much older, including one man that could not have been less than eighty. And standing beside the old man, to the centurion's surprise, was a young child.

The Roman centurion's eyes alone revealed his grim reaction to the sight of the boy, who looked to be no more than six or seven. The centurion knew the vile mob would almost certainly have killed this boy along with the rest. "By all the gods..." he muttered to himself.

For the first time since being hit by Severus' stone, the girl's brother, momentarily regaining consciousness, opened his eyes and spoke, though his words were weak. "Sir, this is our younger brother. As you can see, he is only a child. Please...please, I beg you—"

"Don't talk. You should save your strength." He looked intently at the boy, and at the other Christians. The wind and rain beat fiercely upon their weary faces, giving them the appearance of condemned ghosts, and the centurion felt pity for them. "You have nothing to fear. I am not about to have the murder, or even the arrest, of one so young on my conscience. Your brother may go free. But tell him to leave at once."

The girl knelt beside the boy. "You must go now. It's all right—don't cry. Tell Father what has happened, and that he must on no account try to save us: someone must be there to care for you. Do you understand?"

The boy nodded, but tears were streaming freely down his face. "I don't want you to go," he said in a broken voice.

His sister's eyes were also filled with tears. "I know. But God is King. He will care for us. And we will meet again, whatever happens. You believe this?"

"Yes."

Struggling for consciousness, the wounded man spoke once more. "Godspeed, little brother. We suffer for Christ's sake. I love you." He fainted again.

The girl took her younger brother in her arms. "Courage, dear, like a brave little warrior."

The boy was sobbing now. "I love you. Both of you."

"I love you, too, Hippolytus."

Before Hippolytus ran off, he glanced to the shadows behind the soldiers, for he thought he saw something moving. A flash of lightning revealed the evil countenance of a man with a black patch over one eye—the man who had thrown the stone that hurt Hippolytus' brother. The lightning passed, again hiding the face in darkness, and Hippolytus ran off. But in that moment, the image of that face was burned forever in Hippolytus' memory, and he learned at once to hate it.

As the soldiers began to lead their captives away, Severus, hidden in the shadows, leaned back against the wall, breathing heavily. He straightened the patch on his eye, which had nearly come off in the struggle and confusion. Had anyone seen his face they would have noted a look of anger and bewilderment. Though it may not have been evident why, it was plain that the night's events had not gone quite as he had expected, and it had little to do with the interruption by the soldiers. Whatever it may have been, he was shocked and confused, far more than even the Christians, who had come to expect such violence. He slid into the deeper shadows on the other side of the road and disappeared.

***

Twenty-five years later, Hippolytus walked hastily through the city streets, glancing at the sky as he went. Large drops of water began to fall from the dark clouds above, splashing on the stone pavement and on his head. Hippolytus quickened his pace, not because he disliked rain, for in fact he didn't, but because he wanted to get to the church as soon as possible. The Bishop was ill again—very ill, this time. In fact, if what he had heard was true, the Bishop may very well be...

No, thought Hippolytus to himself. He can't be dying. Not now. We need him. God would not deprive us of his guidance. Not now! His walk became a brisk jog, and then a run. Thunder boomed overhead, and the rain fell harder. He reached the crest of a high hill, where the houses and buildings were beginning to become fewer, drawing farther apart. There was the church, rising into sight not far away, and he slowed his step. A wealthy magistrate had converted to the Christian faith and given his own money to build the church. It was small, but beautiful—better accommodations than most Christians enjoyed. The edge of the city was visible some half a mile away, and beyond it, the joining of the two rivers—the Rhone, from the east, and the Saone, from the north, that marked the setting of Lyons. But the church stood proudly between the rivers, as if commanding and sustaining their glad union. As he looked on the church, his breathing calmed, and he chided himself for his lack of faith. You are a fool, Hippolytus. He must die some day. Why not now? God is King. The Bishop himself would be angry at any suggestion that Christ could not build His Church without him.

The rain was now a downpour but Hippolytus stopped and stood motionless, his black hair drenched and dripping, his clothes soaked to the skin. The church stood, tall and strong, before his eyes—a formidable reminder that it was

14

God's own strength that upheld His people. Yes, he thought to himself. The church will live and prevail. But oh, how shall I endure without Irenaeus? My father in the Faith, my teacher, my guide, my dear friend…

He breathed a prayer of repentance. Lord, you are my true Father, Teacher, Sovereign Guide; the Friend that is closer than a brother. Forgive me, God. And— if this is indeed the hour in which Irenaeus must taste the bitter drink of death—give grace to him…and to us.

Hippolytus began walking again. He thought of Irenaeus, and of all he had meant to the Christian Church. No one was more loved and revered. Irenaeus was the great Scholar and Theologian, who defended the flock of Christ from heresy and false doctrine. He was the Saint among saints: the Pastor, the Peacemaker who sought to hold the church together amid disputes. He had seen the believers of Lyons through many difficult times, though none more trying than the persecutions that had arisen under the emperor Marcus Aurelius twenty-five years earlier—the persecutions that had found Hippolytus' brother and sister on a stormy night.

As Caesar of the Roman Empire, Marcus Aurelius had generally continued the practice of earlier Roman rulers: Christians were not to be sought out, but if publicly accused, they must be forced to renounce their faith, or die. But in some of the cities in Gaul—including Lyons, where Irenaeus and Hippolytus lived—the people had suddenly turned against Christians, and the persecutions had appeared like a bolt of lightning. Many believers in Christ were killed—including Hippolytus' brother and sister. His brother had died that night from the wound inflicted by Severus' stone, but Hippolytus' sister had been tortured, and finally killed, for she would not deny Christ. Hippolytus never saw them again.

Many lost loved ones in those days. Because of the sudden fury of the persecutions, some believers weakened, and denied their faith. But others stood firm, bringing the wrath of the governor and the bloodthirsty mob down upon them. One believer, a man named Sanctus, had been tortured without mercy, and when questioned, would only reply, "I am a Christian." His valour, and that of many others, gave renewed hope and courage to the church. Indeed, some who had at first denied Christ and had been released actually returned to face the governor again—to confess the Faith and give their lives for their Lord. In the first wave of persecutions the noble Pothinus, first Bishop of Lyons, had been slain. Irenaeus was away in Rome or doubtless—as an elder of the church—he too would have perished. Upon his return he had been elected Bishop to replace Pothinus.

Hippolytus reached the church. He made his way inside to a narrow antechamber. At the end of the corridor a door stood partly open. He knocked gently. A face appeared, not much younger than Hippolytus' own, on the other side of the door. The eyes were grey and the hair a reddish-brown. A thin beard surrounded the trembling lips.

"Hippolytus," came a voice, though the face barely moved, so constant was its dismal expression.

"I came as soon as I heard," said Hippolytus. "Is he...?"

"No, he lives," said the other. "But he is very ill. I fear for his life."

"God's will," said Hippolytus. "If it is the Bishop's time to die, the Lord will comfort us. But I must see him now."

"Of course. Please come in," said the grey-eyed man, and Hippolytus entered the chambers. It was a plain room, for the most part, though the mantle above the fireplace was rather ornate and very beautifully carved from a single piece of oak. In the very centre of the room was a large wooden table covered with scrolled parchments, a candle, several bottles of ink, and three quill pens. On the left stood a smaller table bearing a cloak, two hats, a knobby and battered walking stick, and several more parchments. The room's only window overlooked a bed to the right, and on the bed, gazing out the window into the storm, there lay an old man.

Hippolytus walked over to the old man, and knelt

beside him. "Greetings, Master Irenaeus," he said in a soft voice. "How is it with you?"

Irenaeus turned his head and smiled, and to Hippolytus' surprise, pushed himself up on his elbows. "I am well, Hippolytus. And how is it with you?" His voice was ancient, and his face wrinkled, but his demeanor was inconsistent with these signs of age. He now sat up and clapped Hippolytus rather vigorously on the shoulder. Then he began to laugh.

Hippolytus nearly fell over, both from astonishment and from the old man's hearty slap. The grey-eyed man almost dropped a jug of water as he rushed to the bedside.

"Master!" said Hippolytus. "Are you...? Forgive me, I thought——"

Irenaeus interrupted him. "You thought I lingered at Death's Door only to say farewell." He smiled again.

Hippolytus' shock and concern was beginning to melt into a surprised joy. "Indeed, Master, I was led to believe there was reason to think so."

The elderly Bishop shook his head. "The business of the Christian is in one sense nothing else than to be ever preparing for death. I have been ill; it is true. And perhaps there is some reason for concern——I am an old man, Hippolytus." He glanced at the young man who had let Hippolytus in. "Or perhaps the severity of my condition was somewhat exaggerated?"

The grey-eyed man hung his head. Irenaeus smiled at him. "Then again, I suppose my own nephew is bound to feel more keenly than others both responsibility and distress. In truth, I could not manage without him."

Irenaeus' nephew looked up with gratitude, but there were tears in his eyes.

"Then you are not...not dying, Master?" Hippolytus asked with hope in his heart.

"No, as far as I know I am not. I have a year or two left in me, I believe. Death may assume another guise when he comes to my door." His face darkened momentarily. "Or that of any of us," he added in a low voice which the others did not quite hear. "But now," he said, much louder "let us talk, Hippolytus."

The nephew picked up some extra linen from the bed and moved to the door. "I will leave you for an hour, Uncle," he said. "Hippolytus, come for me if he needs anything."

"I will."

The young man left and closed the door. Hippolytus was again surprised as the aged Bishop rose from his bed unaided, and walked over to the table where his pen and parchments lay. He sat at the table and thumbed through the papers for several minutes. Finally, he lifted one of them from among the others. "Ah, here it is," he said. "I called for you, Hippolytus, not to bid you farewell, but to tell you a story."

"A story, sir?"

"Yes, my son. Please sit here, by the fire. There is no need to continue kneeling by the bedside. It is a long tale, of which you know only a part. I now wish you to hear a more complete account."

"I am at your service, Master Irenaeus," said Hippolytus.

"Good." He paused a moment, looking at the door. "My dear nephew is my helper, my right arm in many ways. He cares for me better than I deserve though he worries and frets like an old nursemaid. But you, Hippolytus: you are my disciple, my true son in the Faith, and my friend."

The younger man only looked at the floor.

"To you," continued Irenaeus, "I have entrusted the legacy of the Faith—the doctrine handed down to me from my teachers. You have both the mind and the heart of a scholar, of a pastor. Perhaps, in the Providence of God, you shall serve as an elder or bishop when I am gone. But Hippolytus —you and I may find that God has another plan for us, another way to serve Him and bear witness to His truth."

Hippolytus glanced up, and the Bishop looked hard at his young disciple. "A Storm is brewing, Hippolytus. We have faced storms in the past. You know that as well as any.

But I fear nowhere in the Empire will be safe from the breaking of this tempest. And so, I would tell you of one who faced the Storm, and who weathered it, though he did not survive it."

Hippolytus pondered that remark for a few moments. The old man closed his eyes, and his voice grew quiet, almost reverent. "His name was Polycarp."

The Mirror of Memory

Ephesus, Asia Minor, Anno Domini 100

The wind blew with determination through the town of Ephesus. Merchants and buyers tried to go about their business but a reckless gust sent a fruit stand tumbling, spawning a heated argument between the gruff merchant, and a squeaky-voiced customer who demanded a refund on the apples that had been ruined in the accident.

Through the disarray came the strong stride of a young man of about thirty years of age. His hair was long, and straight, and his beard thin but even. His eyes were a deep black and his garments simple and unadorned. Under one arm he carried a thick, rolled parchment which he held onto tightly as he jumped over the toppled fruit stand. A cat, caught in the middle of all the activity, was obliged to leap quickly out of the way and onto the back of the unfortunate merchant (who shouted and jumped accordingly). If anyone who knew the young man had seen this behaviour, they would have been surprised. His lack of sympathy for the poor merchant was not like him at all.

Perhaps they would have understood, though, if they had known that he was on his way to the deathbed of a dear friend. Tears stained the young man's face as he hastened through the windy streets. In a world where a man of forty was getting along in years, and a man of sixty was an antique, the young man's dying friend – now well over eighty – was something of a miracle. And his coming death, though sorrowful, was not unexpected. They had known this might soon happen so the young man steeled himself – determined that, though he should mourn, still he would not mourn as those without hope. If only he could get there in time, to speak to his friend, to hear once more his wisdom, and to receive his blessing, that would be enough.

He thought he could face the grief if only God would allow him that.

As he rounded a corner, a blast of wind nearly tossed him in the street, but he suddenly found himself supported by the strong arms of another. The young man, winded from his rapid trek across Ephesus, gasped for breath, and looked up to see who had caught him. To his surprise he found, first that the other man's eyes were also filled with tears, and second, that he recognized him.

"Papias!" the young man exclaimed.

"Polycarp!" said the other. "Thank God I've found you. Have you heard?"

Polycarp's eyes searched the face of Papias for any news. "I received your message and came immediately." A sudden fear gripped him. "Don't tell me – Papias, he's not..."

Papias nodded grimly. "Just a few minutes ago. I'm sorry, my friend."

Polycarp fell to his knees. "Oh, God, no! Papias—" Papias lifted his friend from the street, and embraced him. They wept bitterly, for they had both been close to the old man. Polycarp's heart was breaking. All he had wanted was to see him once more, to say farewell to one who had been like a second father to him. But he was now too late. He, who had prayed for courage, who had been determined not to lose hope, now found both courage and hope flying like cowards before the storm of battle.

Still, he gathered his strength as best he could, and followed Papias to the house where their friend had died. They entered, and were greeted by several friends and elders of the church of Ephesus. Papias led Polycarp to a small room, and they went inside. One or two others were there, but they thoughtfully left the room, giving the new arrivals some time alone with the departed loved one.

The old man's body lay on a bed by the window. He looked even older than he really was, but still peaceful and wise, Polycarp noted. Polycarp set the book he had been carrying on a table, and Papias and he sat down in chairs by the bedside. For a long time, neither spoke. A fire crackled in the hearth, and the wind beat mournfully against the tiny home. Finally, Polycarp broke the silence, but his voice was hoarse and quiet.

"I thought I had all the answers. I read Paul's letters to the church at Thessalonica. 'Don't grieve as those who have no hope,' he said. 'Our hope is in Christ. So when sorrow finds us, it does not find us in despair.' Foolishly, I thought I had prayed enough, studied enough, meditated enough that when this moment came, I would be above it; that I would mourn, but not despair."

"But now," replied Papias, "you find that is not the case?"

Polycarp sighed, "Whether I am in despair or not, I know not. But I cannot imagine despair being much worse." He looked again at the dead body before him. The reality and enormity of the loss began to sink in, for this was John himself. John, the evangelist, the follower of Christ. John, known as "the disciple whom Jesus loved". John, the prophet and preacher, John, the storyteller who had written with his own hand of the words and deeds of Christ; John the Eyewitness who had seen and heard and known Jesus, who had walked with Him and watched Him work miracles. John, to whom Jesus had entrusted His own mother; John, who alone remained at the Cross when all others had fled.

"John," said Polycarp in a whisper, his eyes closed. "The last of the apostles of Christ. I cannot believe this Day has come." He put his head in his hands, thinking of the sorrows and trials of the last few years. The church had endured yet another persecution. All had suffered but none more so than John and the other Disciples.

"Do you know," Polycarp said, "as great as the loss of John is to me, there is something else that troubles my heart almost as much as his death?"

"Oh? What's that?"

"Well," said Polycarp, unsure how to put his feelings into words, " how long have we known John, Papias?"

"Nearly fifteen years, I think."

"Fifteen years?" said Polycarp. "I should have thought longer. But for all that time, while I dreaded the loss of our dear teacher — who was already old even when we first came to know him — I always thought that his death would be different."

"What do you mean?"

"John often spoke of those who gave their lives for Christ. He spoke most feelingly, as I recall, of Peter, and of his brother, James, but of others as well — indeed all the other apostles were slain for their loyalty to Christ. In our speech together, he called them martyrs. Of these martyrs he spoke with love, and honor."

"Yes," said Papias, remembering. "He talked of them as being crowned with glory. 'The martyr's crown,' he called it."

"The martyr's crown — yes, that was it," said Polycarp. "And ever since, I have been filled with a desire to wear that crown myself. Not," he added, "because I think myself worthy. I tried to put it out of my mind, for I am no apostle, but I cannot deny the desire that fills my heart."

"I see," said Papias, "and now you are troubled because John himself was denied the crown and honor of a noble death."

Polycarp nodded. "I do not understand why he, alone of the apostles, should be refused."

"And," said Papias, "you fear that if it was not granted to John to wear the martyr's crown, how shall you hope to win it?"

Polycarp nodded again, and there were tears in his eyes, but he spoke no word in answer. Both were silent for a time. Polycarp looked again at his teacher. The tears spilled over onto his cheeks. "What shall we do, Papias?" he said at last. His eyes closed as he attempted to pray.

Papias stood and walked over to the fire. His hair, like that of his friend's, fell to his shoulders, but it was curly, and though he was the same age as Polycarp — only a few weeks younger, in fact — there was already a touch of grey on his head and beard. He was several inches taller than Polycarp, and powerfully built. His skin was deeply tanned from years of working outdoors, and his green eyes shone like emeralds in his dark, intelligent face.

He was a strong man, in body and mind, and though he grieved for John's death, he would not be crushed by it. He had served for a number of years in the Roman army, and though his time in the legions was over, he still thought and acted like a soldier – tough and practical, though not without compassion. He had seen some of the world's worst sorrows, and survived them. He was gifted at encouraging and strengthening others, at providing a strong arm for the weak, and he could see that Polycarp was now in need of such strength.

"Polycarp, my friend," he said, picking up an iron poker from the hearth, "we knew this day would come. This is what it is like to be a Christian when the days of the apostles are over. The apostles told us of Christ and God's word. They were the Keepers of a great Fire – a Fire that warmed hearts, burned consciences, and gave light to the World. But the apostles did not start the Fire, my friend. They merely tended it. The Flame itself lives on. The source of the word of God is not the apostles but the Lord Christ Himself."

A weak smile crept onto Polycarp's face as he noted, not for the first time, that Papias – though a warrior at heart – was not lacking in spiritual wisdom. Indeed, he recognized in Papias' words the unmistakable voice of John himself. That was the sort of thing John would have said.

Papias continued. "The apostles are gone. This is harder for us than for believers yet unborn, for we knew some of them. We are among a blessed few among all believers, of all time, who actually knew them, talked with them, ate with them, learned from them. John, especially, was our teacher and spiritual father. And like a good father, he did not leave his children without a legacy."

Polycarp looked with sadness at the still face on the bed. "What legacy, Papias?"

Papias smiled, "We have the legacy of memory."

"Memory?" exclaimed Polycarp with scorn. "That is no legacy. Memory is only like a dim reflection in a muddy pool or a dirty mirror. I would rather have one more hour with this great man than murky memories."

Polycarp rose and walked to the window. On the ground below, a wooden barrel was still nearly filled with last week's rains. Polycarp glanced into the water and saw his own reflection staring back.

"Mirrors and memories," he muttered to himself. And yet, as he looked at the image in the water, hazy and distorted by the new raindrops falling into the barrel, it brought to mind something he had heard once, long ago, if only he could remember. What was it? Something about mirrors, and their dim reflections.

It came to him. "Now we see in a mirror, dimly," he said, still gazing into the water, "but then face to face."

Papias' eyes had been fixed on the fire but Polycarp's words roused him from his reverie. "Hmm? What's that?"

"Something the Apostle Paul said: 'Now we see in a mirror, dimly, but then face to face.' He was talking about our knowledge and understanding of God, and how, when Christ returns, we will know Him as fully and completely as is possible for men to know. But here, now, we only see Him as it were in a mirror. A dim reflection of the truth."

"Yes, I remember that. Interesting words, especially coming from one who had actually seen and conversed with Jesus."

"Indeed. John told me of Paul's words, long before I read them for myself. I suppose he's right. When Christ returns, a clearer picture will emerge. But for now, we see what we have been given to see."

Papias smiled, and Polycarp drew closer to the fire. "Come," said Polycarp. "Memory is indeed a fine legacy. But John's legacy was greater than that–he bequeathed Christ himself to us, Papias. For a little while, let us forget our grief and remember the stories. Let us unpack the treasure-trove of memory, and see what jewels lie within."

For more than an hour, Polycarp and Papias reminisced. They recalled, with fondness and sadness their days with John, or stories he had told them of his days with Christ. Polycarp remembered the words that John had shared with them – words that he had heard from Christ himself.

Polycarp and Papias both remained lost in their own thoughts for a while. In those early years they had both learned much from the great apostle and from others like him. He had shown them too that the life of a follower of Christ was marked by many troubles.

Polycarp's eye glanced at some old parchments laid out on a table, letters and writings from friends and believers scattered far and wide. His mind went back to one of those dangerous missions that he and Papias had known so well. They had been given an epistle to deliver to the believers at Rome. 'Do you remember that Papias when John had been in prison at Patmos. We all feared for his life as well as our own, but the two of us were determined to deliver that letter to the believers in Rome.'

Papias nodded, 'But first we had to find them.'

The City of Seven Hills

Rome, Anno Domini 94

It had been a sultry summer night when Polycarp and
Papias had arrived by cart in Rome. Their faces were
hooded, and they kept to the shadows as much as possible.
Polycarp held a thick parchment, rolled and bound, under
his arm. Leaving their horse and rig at a nearby livery, they
shouldered their packs and walked quickly through the city
streets, glancing to either side as they went. Both sensed
that danger lurked behind every shadow, behind every face
they saw, though it seemed that no one took much notice
of them. They had to travel by quite a winding route, along
many alleys and shrouded streets, but always up, ascending
to their destination in the heart of Rome, the city of seven
hills.

By prior arrangement, they made their way down
the main street called the Via Sacra. The road was paved,
and lined with majestic colonnades, and led them up and
up, until at last they reached the Arch of Titus. This was
an imposing structure that spanned the Via Sacra, looking
down on the great city. They were to await someone here,
but since no one was in sight, they took a few moments to
look at the Arch. Domitian, the Roman Emperor, had raised
it several years before, in honor of his brother, Titus and
his conquests in Judea. Titus, who had preceded Domitian
as Caesar, had conquered Jerusalem, and destroyed the
Temple, carrying off the sacred treasures of the Jews as
spoils of war.

The full moon lit the Arch's outer stonework and
inscription with an eerie clarity. They read the inscription
engraved at the crest of the Arch:

Senatus Populusque Romanus Divo Tito Divi
Vespasiani Filio Vespasiano Augusto

"The Roman Senate and People to Deified Titus, Vespasian Augustus, son of Deified Vespasian."

The Romans revered their dead emperors as gods.

The two friends walked under the archway, squinting their eyes to see the beautifully carved relief sculptures on the inside walls. One image in particular drew their attention: a triumphant procession of Romans bearing aloft the sacred treasures of the Jews: the menorah, the table of Shewbread, and the silver trumpets that had called them to worship on the holy day of Rosh Hashanah.

"A grim picture," said Papais. "A reminder that there is an end that awaits those who defy Rome."

"A grim picture, yes," said Polycarp. "But one of judgment, and a sign that even a pagan empire may be used as a sword in God's hand. For this was prophesied many years ago by our Lord."

They walked through the other side of the Arch and looked down on Rome. Not far away, beyond the Arch to the northwest, rose the great Colosseum, a wonder of Roman architecture. Tall and imposing it rose from the shadows of night, a fearsome sight in many ways. It seemed the entire city was in attendance there, for there was no sign of man or woman on the roads, and the sound of trumpets and the hum of tens of thousands talking at once could be heard from the roofless Colosseum. Polycarp tried to appreciate, if only for a moment, the impressive design and architectural beauty of the Colosseum. But he knew about the dark deeds that went on inside, and sensed that there were even darker deeds to come, so he could find no glory in the sight of this magnificent building.

Papias felt differently for he had been here before. Old memories resurfaced of glorious deeds and of some harsher moments he would rather have forgotten. He knew that though Rome was often cruel and tyrannical, there was still much wonder and beauty in its accomplishments. But he also knew about Rome's brutality. As if in answer to his thoughts, there came from the Colosseum a mighty roar of thousands of voices. Both men shuddered, imagining what terrifying spectacle might have caused such a joyous response from the people of Rome.

Polycarp turned his head to the side. There was another noise, somewhere nearby. It was growing steadily nearer, but what was it? Suddenly, he grabbed Papias and pulled him back behind one of the nearby colonnades.

"What is it, Polycarp?" Papias whispered as they crouched in the darkness.

"Wait," said his friend. Soon both could hear the sound: the noise of many leather boots, marching in time along the paved surface of the Via Sacra. Then the source of the sound came in view: a company of perhaps thirty Roman soldiers marched past them and under the Arch of Titus. They held their breaths, praying silently, knowing that discovery could mean death.

But the soldiers passed on, leaving the two travellers unfound. They remained hidden, listening intently. Somewhere in the distance a dog barked. The noise of the Colosseum could still be heard, but there was no sound of anyone nearby. When some minutes had gone by, they judged the danger had passed. They breathed deeply in relief.

A half hour passed, then an hour. They began to grow doubtful, worried. Still, they remained hidden: all they knew was that the Roman Christians sent messengers to several places around the city—including the Arch of Titus—every third night, in case any believers still needed to find a way into hiding with the rest of the church. This was the night for the messengers to appear, so Polycarp and Papias sat still in the darkness, waiting for a sign, some signal that might tell them who to look for.

The task was easier than they had imagined. Apart from the soldiers, only one man approached the Arch during their wait, and he passed quickly by and disappeared. Then, when they had been hidden for nearly an hour and a half, another man came into view, darkly dressed, but walking casually enough, and carrying a staff. He walked under the arch and glanced at the sculptures within. Then, he came out and stood with his back against the Arch, his eyes peering back down the Via Sacra, in the direction from whence he had come.

There he waited, just across the road from where Polycarp and Papias sat still, barely breathing. They could not see his face. A quarter of an hour passed, and still the stranger made no sign or movement. With a nod of agreement, Polycarp and Papias rose and strode towards him.

Papias stopped short as he saw the man's face, for he recognized him: it was an old friend from his military days, a man Papias knew to have converted to Christ in the years since. They clasped hands fervently, smiling in joy at this unexpected reunion. They discovered quickly enough that this man was indeed the messenger they had been looking for. In minutes, he had shown them the way they should take, and departed on another errand for the Roman church, promising to look for them later. Wrapping their cloaks tighter about themselves, despite the heat, Polycarp and Papias walked on through the night, keeping to side streets and unlit alleyways.

***

Minutes later, Polycarp and Papias were walking back down the Via Sacra, following the course that the Watcher had given them. They glanced back to the Arch of Titus to see if they could descry their guide, but he had already disappeared into the darkness. Wrapping their cloaks tighter about themselves, they walked on through the night, keeping to side streets and unlit alleyways.

Suddenly, a shadowy figure darted from the side of a building, and rammed right into Polycarp. He gave a sharp cry of surprise, but Papias grabbed the attacker, closing his fingers around the shadow's throat. The attacker kicked and punched, but could not break free.

"Don't struggle, or you're dead," said Papias.

Polycarp shivered slightly at his companion's rather ruthless words. Sometimes there was something about

Papias and his fierce nature that made Polycarp feel uneasy. "That's what comes with being one of the Roman army for so long," Polycarp muttered to himself as the attacker, breathing heavily, spoke quickly.

"Let me go — I mean no harm. It was an accident!" To the surprise of the two men, the voice was that of a young girl with jet black hair and piercing dark eyes.

Papias relaxed his grip. He breathed a sigh of relief, despite his astonishment. "What are you doing, running into us like that?" he demanded, firmly.

The girl looked intently into their faces almost as if she were trying to memorize their features, then with surprising strength, and a lightning-fast twist, she wrenched free and sprang away into the night. Papias tried to catch her, but she was too quick. It would have been dangerous and pointless, Papias knew, to waste time looking for her. He shook his head, exhaling in frustration.

"It would have been better had we not been seen."

Polycarp sighed. "It can't be helped. She was just passing by. She doesn't know us, or where we're going."

"I hope you're right."

There was nothing to do but move on as quickly as possible. The moon hid behind a patch of black clouds making their journey a dark one. Leaving the city, they began to walk around it, outside the walls, heading south and then west, watching and listening for signs of pursuit.

They walked on through fields of tall grass and scattered trees. In a little under half an hour, they came to their destination: a barely discernible track leading down to a narrow ravine overshadowed with trees and bushes. They made their way down this hidden pathway to a place that seemed to have had all light drained from it. They were in total darkness, and their direction seemed uncertain.

For a moment, they were in doubt, but then, high overhead, the clouds parted, and a silver shaft of moonlight pierced the gloom. They looked around them, trying to gain their bearings. The ravine had joined a thin wood, and there were trees on both sides. To the right there was a sort of clearing with a single tree growing right up against the side of one of the hills. They walked up to the tree and, kneeling down beside it, began to look closely at its base.

Soon they found what they were looking for at the roots: a small symbol, painted in red. It was so small that it might never have been noticed unless someone was looking for it. In the dim half-light of the little valley, it was nearly invisible. It appeared to be a tiny wreath of thorns.

"This is the place," said Papias, in a whisper. Polycarp nodded. They cleared away some of the tangled bracken to the right of the tree, and after a few minutes of searching uncovered a small door. They tried the handle, but it was locked. Papias knocked gently, and then waited. Some time passed before footsteps were heard within. Then, the door opened ever so slightly. The men could see nothing inside the black entrance.

Finally, Polycarp spoke. "We are here to see Clement," he said simply.

Still, no reply came. The two men began to glance around wondering where they would go if not welcomed here. At last, a voice whispered from behind the door.

"Your names?"

Polycarp and Papias looked at each other. Suddenly they felt nervous. Should they speak or not? If this were the wrong place, all could be lost. Yet they would never know unless they took the chance. They nodded at each other in silent agreement, and Polycarp spoke again.

"Polycarp of Smyrna, and Papias of Hierapolis."

Another silence. Then, the whispering voice again. "He is risen."

The two visitors spoke together this time, in a whisper that betrayed much relief. "He is risen, indeed!"

Slowly, the door opened inward, but still nothing could be seen of their host. Polycarp and Papias entered, stooping low and pushing their way through the thick bushes that covered the door. With no light inside the doorway the two men were gently led through to a large echoing hallway, with a floor of stone. The way was straight for a while, but soon began to wind to the left, and to slope down.

In only a few minutes, their guide stopped. Apparently they had reached a door, for Polycarp and Papias could hear a faint metallic sound, as of keys on a ring. One key was selected by touch, and inserted into a keyhole. The latch clicked, and the door opened, through which they entered. Once inside, he shut the door, and lit a candle.

They were in a narrow, stuffy room with a door on the far wall. For the first time, they looked into the face of the man who had let them in. He was older than they. His hair was silvery with streaks of black, and his beard was straight and long.

"Please forgive the discourtesy at the door, but we can not open our doors these days without fear. However you may find better hospitality once we reach our destination."

He eyed them closely and smiled. "So," he said at last. "Polycarp of Smyrna and Papias of Hierapolis. Which is which, I wonder? But no, as I have treated you badly, I will speak first. I am Marcus Antonius, generally known as Mark, and an elder in the church of Rome."

Polycarp answered with a bow. "I am Polycarp, and this is Papias, my companion. We are disciples of John the Apostle."

"Ah," said Mark. "Of John, eh? Remarkable man, I hear, though I never met him. I did know Peter, in my youth, if *knowing* is the right word – my father knew him, and I was acquainted with him. But I am eager to hear from those who know 'the disciple whom Jesus loved.' Especially since he's the last Apostle."

Papias nodded. "And at his age, every moment, every word, becomes more precious. That, indeed, is why we have come."

Mark's eyebrows went up. "Oh?"

Papias gestured to Polycarp, who held forth the rolled parchment. "This," he said, "is a letter written by John himself."

Mark's eyes grew wide. "A letter from John? To Clement?"

"No, not exactly," said Polycarp. "This is the Revelation God gave John, then in exile on the island of Patmos, to seven churches in various cities – among them Smyrna, my hometown. We had heard that many of your copies of the Scriptures were lost or destroyed in the persecution, and in the flight to the catacombs. John asked us to bring this letter, and others, to our fellow believers in Rome. Most are copies, but this is the original letter, as we first received it in Smyrna, written by the hand of John himself."

Mark looked at the visitors with a new wonder. "Well, well. We must be off at once. Clement will be glad indeed of this gift, for we have been sorely grieved at the loss of the Scriptures. Come."

Mark lit two torches, and handed one to Polycarp. Then he ushered the two travellers through a door that opened onto a stair that spiralled downwards, always downwards. From time to time, they would reach a sort of landing, from which several rooms would branch off to either side. Polycarp thought he could see glimpses of carved words and painted images on the walls within.

At last, the stairs ended in a chamber, with passages leading off in several directions. Here at last they could see, up close, what they only glimpsed in the other rooms. These were galleries for the burial of the dead – catacombs. Within the rooms, and along the passageways, burial chambers were carved out of rock walls and covered with marble or large tiles set in mortar. On each stone grave was set an inscription, and many paintings adorned them.

"Some were buried here during the persecutions of Nero, many years ago," said Mark, anticipating their question. "But the catacombs have been built upon and improved since that time. For some, seeking a refuge from persecution, they have become a place of temporary rest;

others will rest here much longer, until the end of the world."

They read many of the epitaphs as they walked along. On one marble grave, they read the name:

C. IVLIA. AGRIPPINA

the Latin for, Caia Julia Agrippina. The name of Caia Julia Agrippina was an aristocratic name, but the tombs were those of rich and poor alike – beloved husbands and wives, children, brothers and sisters, deacons and elders of the church, martyrs who had given their lives for Christ. Many of the tombs were embellished with paintings: images of men and women praying; pictures representing the great stories of the Prophets, the Apostles, and Christ Himself; images of ships, bread and wine, fish, a shepherd carrying a lamb on his shoulders.

Soon the passages opened into a wide chamber, which they crossed to find another door. Mark knocked and presently the door was opened by a young woman who led them inside.

"Most everyone is asleep, now," said Mark, as they extinguished their torches "but you were expected, so I was asked to watch the outer door for your arrival."

Mark then led them through a dark corridor past several rooms before stopping at one on the right hand side. He knocked, very gently, on the door.

The door creaked open, and the wise, kindly face of a man appeared. He was perhaps sixty years old. "Ah, Marcus. So you have brought them?"

"I have, sir. This is Papias of Hierapolis, and Polycarp of the city of Smyrna." He turned to the two visitors. "Brothers, this is Clement, our bishop here in Rome."

"Well met, Papias," said Clement. "And Polycarp! We have met before, I think, though it was several years ago. I welcome you both. Come in, please." The three men entered to find a plain, oddly shaped room, almost like a cave, with walls that looked to be made of rock. In the far corner of the room, nearly hidden in the shadows, was a small table or desk. The room was lit by torches on two walls and a candle on a round table in the centre of the room. There were three men sitting at the table. One was gray-haired, and one was bald with a fairly long beard, but the third looked to be older than any of them. His back was slightly bent, and he was dressed in a gray tunic. His hair and beard were completely white, but there was a fierce, bold light in his eyes, and an expression of resolute watchfulness.

His name was Ignatius, Bishop of Antioch in Syria. Papias recognized him at once, for some years ago when Papias was still a young boy he had heard Ignatius teach. Indeed, Ignatius' bold words had influenced both him and his parents to become Christians. Ignatius had been ordained as Bishop of Antioch by Peter himself. But there was another story that both Papias and Polycarp had heard about Ignatius - though no one seemed to know whether it was true. It involved a story from the life of Jesus. On one occasion, when the disciples had been arguing over who among them was the greatest, Jesus took a little child and set him in their midst; then He took him in His arms and said, "If anyone wants to be first, he must be the very last, and the servant of all. Whoever welcomes one of these little children in my name welcomes me; and whoever welcomes me does not welcome me but the one who sent me."

The name of that little child (so said the legend) was Ignatius. Papias felt a strong desire to ask if the legend was true, but it was not the proper time or place.

Polycarp rejoiced to meet Clement once again. They had met in Ephesus several years before when Clement had visited John there. 'A great man,' thought Polycarp as they greeted one another. Polycarp knew that Clement had worked tirelessly in the short time since he had become bishop, for he had come into his stewardship in troubled times. He could not help thinking that Clement's greatest challenges still lay ahead.

Clement nodded towards the parchment strewn table. "Ignatius and the church leaders were met to take council together, to find the wisdom they needed to face the persecution. Come dine with us and we shall eat and talk at the same time. Tell us about your journey. You will have had troubles of your own getting here. The Imperial Edict against Christians makes travel almost impossible."

The fellow believers sat down to a simple fare of cheese, apples, soft bread, some rather dry meat, and a little wine. The travellers were immensely grateful.

"Travel is difficult and dangerous these days," Polycarp continued their conversation. "But what of Rome? The threat is greatest here, as we have heard. What has been happening? What plans do you have to …."

But at that moment, an unexpected voice sounded from across the room.

"Don't tell them anything! They come bearing swords against you! They are spies!"

Escape From Rome

Papias jumped from his chair in surprise, but Polycarp calmly laid a hand on his arm.

"Wait, Papias," he said. "Don't you recognize the voice?"

Papias didn't and looked at his friend with a puzzled expression. Mark stood and began walking around the table. "I recognize it," he said in a strange tone. Stranger still, he walked over to a pile of cloaks and parchments in the corner and began speaking to it.

"Now then," he said in a commanding voice. "What's this all about, eh?"

For a few moments, nothing happened. Then, there was a scuffling noise and the head of a young girl appeared. Her eyes were stern and they looked right at the newcomers.

"Why, Polycarp," said Papias, "that's the same girl – "

"Yes, it is," said Polycarp. "The one from the city."

"Come on out, Lydia," said Mark. The girl's eyes glanced up at him, upon which they softened a little.

"They are spies, Father," she said.

"Yes, you said that," replied Mark. "But what makes you think so?"

"I saw them earlier this evening," she said, as she came out from her hiding place.

"Ran into us in Rome, so to speak," said Papias, who then winced at a well-placed elbow from Polycarp.

"Ran into them?" said Mark, still looking at Lydia.

"It was an accident, Mark," said Polycarp. "The girl ran out from behind a building and bumped into me. No harm was done, but she ran off before we could tell her so."

"I see," said Mark. "But I don't think it was an accident. Was it, Lydia?"

Lydia looked down but did not reply.

"Was it?"

"No, sir."

"What happened, then?"

Lydia looked directly into her father's eyes. "Some of us were playing near the entrance at Caelian Hill. I had heard you saying that we may not be safe much longer, for someone had tried to find us by pretending to be Christians. I – "

"That will do," said Mark. "The rest of the story is plain enough. You slipped away from the others, left the catacombs through the quarry, and have been doing a little spying of your own. You ran into these men to get a better look at them, and then you followed them."

He turned to the guests. "My daughter has more courage than many men I have known, though it sometimes causes her to forget her duty of obedience."

Here he looked at Lydia again. "Going into the city like that was foolish and dangerous, and it is a wonder you were not caught. Your actions will have consequences, as you know."

"Yes, Father. But I still say they are spies."

"Why?"

"They carry swords. I've never met a Christian who carries a sword. Why else would they have them if not to use them against us?"

Polycarp smiled. "I'm afraid you are mistaken, O lady of valour. We carry no swords, other than the Sword of Scripture, which all Christians should bear."

Papias coughed gently. "Polycarp," he said. "That isn't quite true. I am wearing a sword. Young Lydia must have seen it when I caught her."

Polycarp was astonished. "What? Why have you kept this from me? How is it that we have travelled together for hundreds of miles and I did not know? And why do you have such a thing in the first place?"

Papias sighed, "I kept it from you because I knew you would not approve. You did not know about it because I have some skill in keeping secrets, even over hundreds of miles. And as to why I have it...let us just say I have it because I judged there is need for it. But perhaps this would be better discussed later, my friend."

Polycarp looked troubled but he agreed. Clement stood and spoke. "Lydia, a sword does not of necessity mark a man as an enemy. But if doubts linger, my child, there is a way to be certain. Polycarp, I believe you brought something for us?"

Polycarp turned his gaze from his friend. "Yes, Bishop Clement, I have." He brought out the parchment he had carried so far. "This," he said as he handed it to the Roman bishop, "is the original letter chronicling John's Revelation give to him by Christ himself on Patmos. It is one of several copies of the Holy Writings of the Apostles that we have brought to replace those that Roman persecution has stolen from you. This is our token – a sign that we are not enemies."

The faces of the gathered elders and even Lydia showed astonishment and wonder.

"You see, Lydia?" said Clement. "A letter from the last of the Apostles. Master Ignatius and I know John well enough to know whether this is his writing. So we will examine this letter, and if it is genuine, we will accept these men as brothers.

"If not," he added with a smile, "we will scold them soundly and bend our knees to Lydia in contrition. What do you say?"

Lydia's face still seemed uncertain, but she nodded in agreement. "Though if it is not genuine, it is already too late," she muttered, "and we must all prepare to face the sword of Papias."

Papias smiled with genuine admiration for her courage.

Clement unrolled the parchment. He and Ignatius read it closely for some minutes, speaking in soft voices to one another. At last they raised their heads.

"Well, Ignatius," said Clement. "What say you? Shall we open our arms to these men, or praise the watchful eyes of brave Lydia?"

The elderly bishop rose and put his hand on Lydia's head. "We shall do both," he said. "For this is assuredly the hand of John, and no other. Yet Lydia's courage is a reminder to all of us of the real danger that we are in, and that we must be ready."

The others raised their cups in assent. Lydia smiled. Clement gave his approval of Ignatius' assessment of the letter, and they all sat down.

"We must spend some time reading this letter tonight," Clement exclaimed. "I have missed these words of John, and I cannot thank you enough for bringing them to us. You have encouraged me greatly. But first, let us speak of darker matters. Polycarp, Papias — we thank you for the pains and dangers you have endured to bring this to us. I fear more perils lie ahead for us all.

"You know that Ignatius came to visit the family of a great friend of his who died last year. He stayed to help his fellow believers in dark days. He journeyed alone, for he judged it better to leave his church in Antioch well tended in his absence. He has been a joy and a strength to Rome during the last few months. And since the persecutions began he has helped set up this underground church and has done such valiant deeds as are rarely seen.

"But it is time for him to depart. Not by our choice, for we will be sorry to see him go. But Domitian has made it a crime to follow Christ. The persecution has intensified here, and is now moving steadily throughout the Empire. Ignatius longs to return to his flock, to protect them and to encourage them. The least that we owe him is to see him safely on his way.

"But you see the difficulty, brothers? While the church here lasts, it is our duty as elders to stay with it until the end, whatever perils we must face. The others here have families, and they are duty-bound to protect them."

"And that is why, gentlemen," said Ignatius, "you must

let me depart alone. God will see me safely to my home, if it is His will."

Clement smiled grimly. "Ignatius would have already left, alone, had we not insisted that he remain until we can decide what to do. Perhaps I shouldn't say this, but one of our elders has already offered to accompany Ignatius on his way, though it would grieve him deeply to leave his family in such dangerous days. He is willing to go if no other guide can be found."

Papias thought he saw Clement glance quickly at Mark as he said this.

Clement continued. "We have not decided what is best to do. It will not be easy to get out of Rome. Indeed I am rather amazed that you got in, though I suppose it is always easier to get in a prison than to get out."

"Master Clement," said Polycarp suddenly. "Forgive my interruption." He looked with deep feeling at the faces before him. "To be here with all of you is more honor than I will ever deserve. But Papias and I cannot remain here. We must also return to our homes and loved ones. Perhaps this is the reason that God sent us here to Rome?"

Papias nodded. "Polycarp is right. We learned much on our journey, and know the safest roads to travel. We can provide guidance and perhaps a measure of protection for Master Ignatius."

Clement smiled again. "I would not have asked this of you, my friends. But since you offer so graciously, I will tell you plainly that I believed from the beginning that God sent you here for this, and that your choice is right."

He turned to Ignatius. "Well, Master," he said. "What do you say? Will you travel alone?"

Ignatius began to laugh quietly. "You have won me, Clement," he said. "And I thank you for your concern and your gracious hospitality during these trying times. I am grateful too for the offer of company on the road, good sirs," he said to Polycarp and Papias. "I hope that some of our journey at least, will be peaceful enough to allow me to get to know you both better."

Polycarp and Papias stood and bowed. "Sir, the honor is entirely ours," said Papias.

Ignatius smiled.

***

They made their plans for departure, and spent the next several hours reading John's letter to the churches. Even little Lydia listened for a long while, until she fell asleep in her father's arms sometime after midnight.

It was decided that they would set out at night ten days later. There was to be a magnificent gladiatorial combat in the Colosseum, and it seemed that everyone, from the lowly servant, to the wealthy aristocrat, even the Emperor himself, was planning to be there. There would be no better chance to slip away unnoticed, under cover of darkness.

But there had been news that Domitian had posted guards at various points around the outside wall of the city, in an attempt to capture Christians coming and going from their various catacomb entrances. The night before the planned escape, Clement received word that three of the Emperor's Praetorians, the elite Imperial guard, had taken a post only a short distance from the catacomb door through which Polycarp and Papias had entered. There seemed, however, to be no guards in the area of the Caelian Hill entrance so it was decided that they would leave their hiding place that way.

On the appointed night, a short while after the fights got under way at the Colosseum, Polycarp, Papias, and Ignatius prepared to depart. In the short time of their visit to the Roman Church, they had developed a surprisingly strong friendship with the faithful band of believers there. The parting therefore, left their hearts heavy. Papias had grown rather attached to Lydia, the valiant little girl who had thought he was a spy. She tried not to cry when they left, but she could not hide the tears that welled up when it was time to say farewell.

"Goodbye, Lydia," said Papias, softly. "Your courage is a gift, you know. Be thankful, and use it well."

"I will. Goodbye, Papias."

Mark, as well as many of the other believers, bade them farewell with many blessings and promises of prayers for a safe journey. It was a difficult parting when the church said farewell to Ignatius, for he had lifted their hearts just when they needed it most.

Clement offered a prayer for safety and blessing before they set out. He gave Polycarp a letter of thanks for John; then Polycarp and Papias turned and walked up the stairs to the gallery opening that led to the streets of Rome.

***

Careful planning of the escape route proved to be invaluable. They had chosen the perfect time. With the help of Clement and other believers who knew Rome well, they were able to make their way out of the door at Caelian Hill and across Rome to the western side of the city. The journey was tense but uneventful. They moved as quickly as they could without compromising their safety, keeping away from the main roads. Their plan was to journey by river in a boat owned by one of the believers. They found it, tied to a dock just where they had been told that it would be, and began to untie it. Papias had barely laid his hand on the rope when a clear, strong voice broke the silence.

"Who are you? What are you about?" The three men whirled around in surprise. They were out of the shadows now, the light of the moon was bright, and they were completely visible. There before them, not thirty feet away, stood a Roman soldier carrying a javelin and a large shield. A sword gleamed at his side and his face was stern.

"A Praetorian," gasped Papias. "Get in the boat, now!" he shouted to his companions. In an instant, his sword was out, and he brought it down in a sweeping blow on the rope, severing it cleanly. Polycarp leapt into the boat, then quickly helped Ignatius in, but the Praetorian was running at them at full speed. He had dropped his javelin and drawn his sword. Papias began to push the boat into the water, but the soldier was nearly on top of them. Papias' back was to the Praetorian but he instinctively swung his sword around just in time to meet his opponent's blow. The shattering ring of steel on steel cut the still air.

"In the name of the Emperor, lay down your weapon!" the soldier shouted as both he and Papias reeled backward from the impact. Papias could see that the man was young. Too young for a Praetorian, Papias thought, sizing him up in an instant. Must be a fledgling military prodigy. But youth had its disadvantages as well.

Papias moved forward, sword at the ready. It seemed that he heard the voice of Polycarp, shouting to stop, but it was distant, as if he were calling from across the river. Again, the soldier lunged at his opponent, taking him for a common criminal. Papias met the blow, and the swords clashed again and again, the sound echoing in the night air, competing with the now distant noise of the Colosseum.

Twisting his body to deflect a well-aimed blow, Papias lost his balance and fell hard to the ground.

"No!" cried Polycarp as he jumped from the boat to Papias' aid, Ignatius following right behind him. But the Praetorian's over-handed kill stroke missed its mark as Papias rolled out of the way just in time. The sword plunged deep into the soft earth.

Polycarp was now between Papias and the Praetorian. The young warrior pulled his sword from the ground and with a swift move pressed it against Polycarp's neck.

Ignatius spoke quickly, intervening on behalf of his friend. "Wait, do not do this. I am Ignatius, a leader of the Christian Church. Take me. I am the one you want."

There was a deathly gleam in the soldier's eyes, and anger. "I know what I want. I have orders to kill all such dissenters who will not come peaceably."

"I will come peaceably. Only let these men go."

"No bargains, old man. You have already failed to come peaceably. Thus you die." Ignatius could see that he was serious. The soldier pressed the sword on Polycarp, drawing blood as he did so.

Ignatius' voice sounded with a commanding ring. "Release him!"

But the Praetorian made no answer. There was a flash of metal in the moonlight. Then a sickening thud, and Papias' sword, perfectly thrown, lodged deep in the Praetorian's chest, pushing in the leather breastplate with the force of the mighty blow.

The Praetorian gasped for air, only for a few moments, before falling dead. As he fell, the edge of his sword ran across Polycarp's neck, drawing more blood. Polycarp gasped, stunned and shaken.

"God have mercy," he said in a hoarse whisper. He fell to his knees. Ignatius and Papias were by his side in a moment. They quickly treated his neck as well as they could, and Papias' hand as well – he had got the wound by deflecting the Praetorian's sword with his bare hand, a move that saved his life.

"And now, into the boat!" said Papias.

Polycarp's head was swimming and he felt sick. "But – what about him?" he asked, looking down at the fallen warrior.

"He is dead," said Papias. "We can do nothing for him. But we have a task before us: to lead the Bishop to safety. The noise of the fight will soon bring others to investigate. We must go now!" He jumped into the boat, and helped his companions in. Papias moved with the determined action of a man who had seen, and perhaps done, far worse things than this. But Polycarp moved as one in a dream – or a nightmare, for he was shocked by the sudden turn of events, and even more shocked that it was his friend Papias who had done what he saw as a rash and fearful deed.

Polycarp and Papias paddled the boat, moving with the current, away from the lights of Rome. None spoke. Papias gazed ahead while listening for sounds of pursuit. Polycarp's head was down, barely noticing where they were going. Ignatius glanced back at the dwindling lights as the river bore them swiftly south, away from the city of seven hills, away from the city of Rome.

By the Sword

The heat was oppressive, even with no sun in the sky. The three men drove the boat on with as much speed as possible, trying to get far away from Rome before resting. For two hours they laboured, sweating and breathing heavily in the warm summer air. Exhaustion burdened their aching limbs with a stony heaviness.

At length, a fine, gentle rain began to fall, and a wind from the north filled their sails, pushing them forward, and allowing them to rest for a while. They welcomed the cool rain, letting it ease their hot limbs and faces. Ignatius fell asleep in the stern of the boat. No one spoke for quite a long time. Well over an hour later, as they ran on before the wind, Polycarp gave voice to thoughts that had occupied his mind since they left Rome.

"Papias," he said quietly.

"Yes?"

"My heart is heavy for the young man we left by the river in Rome, and I would speak to you about it."

"All right. Say on."

Polycarp sighed and considered his words before continuing. "You deceived me. You did not tell me you bore a hidden weapon, nor did you ever reveal your thoughts about it. Why? Because you knew I would not approve, as you yourself said."

"That is true."

"I thought our friendship was strong enough to endure such disputes. You should have told me."

Papias looked back at his friend with a hint of regret in his eyes. "You are right, Polycarp. I should have told you. But it seemed unwise to burden you with something that I

47

knew would only trouble you. I see now I have not avoided that." Papias sighed. "But you saw what happened? Was I not right to be concerned?"

Polycarp's eyes flashed with a moment of anger. "We knew dangers lay on every side, Papias. The fact that those dangers found us does not justify your actions."

"Then what would you have had me do?"

Polycarp started to answer but said nothing. Yet Papias thought he understood his friend's thoughts well enough without having to hear the words. "You believe I am wrong to bear a sword at all, even to defend my own life, or that of my friends," he declared.

Polycarp looked at him steadily. "Yes, I do."

"Why?"

"You are not the first to take up arms in defense of friends. Peter himself drew his blade in defense of One far worthier than I."

Papias nodded. "Jesus. In the Garden of Gethsemane, the night he was betrayed."

"You are well-versed in the Sacred Scriptures and nothing is hidden from you. I will not ask if you recall Jesus' words to Peter when he struck the servant of the High Priest, for I know you do."

"Of course: 'Put your sword back into its place. For all who take the sword will perish by the sword.' I remember those words well," said Papias, "and I have often pondered them. But Christ said other things. 'I have not come to bring peace, but a sword.'"

"He was speaking poetically, Papias. Don't you understand that?"

"I do. He meant that people would be divided because of Him. As far as I know, He never carried a sword. Very well, it's a small point. But there are other things. On the same night He was betrayed did He not say, 'let the one who has no sword sell his cloak, and buy one'?"

Polycarp was silent for a moment. These words were indeed known to him, but he had long forgotten them. What did they mean?

Papias continued. "The disciples said, 'Lord, behold, here are two swords.' They didn't clean their fish with those swords, Polycarp – they were made to kill."

"Then why did Jesus rebuke Peter later that night for using one?"

"Probably for one or two reasons. First, His words regarding the sword meant that they would need to provide for their protection on their journeys, not that they should take up the sword as aggressors. But also because the Son of God was on His way to the Cross – to defeat the Devil, secure forgiveness for His people, and destroy the power of Death. He was about to wage war, as surely as if He had taken up a sword, but it was a conflict that could only be won by His own death. Peter's impulse was right – to defend righteousness against the wicked. But Jesus stopped Him because this was a unique night, and a unique mission: one that He must not be hindered from accomplishing."

Polycarp sighed. "I don't know, Papias. It strikes me as a lack of trust in God. Did not Jesus teach us to pray, 'Deliver us from evil'? Are we not to trust Him to do so?"

"Yes," said Papias. "He also taught us to pray, 'Give us this day our daily bread,' but we are not to stop working to provide that bread for our families. Think of Nehemiah's words: 'Remember the Lord, who is great and awesome, and fight for your brothers, your sons, your daughters, your wives, and your homes.'"

Both were silent for some minutes. At length, Polycarp spoke again.

"Papias, your words have given me much to think about. But the words of Christ – 'All who take the sword will perish by the sword' – they seem broader to me than just Peter's actions that one night. He is giving a standard, a truth by which to live. We can trust God, or we can take our destinies into our own hands, willing our own safety and protection, even when it may not be His will. Surely Peter might have taken up the sword again, and saved his own life, years later, when he was imprisoned and murdered by Nero. Paul, or James, or any of the others who have been slain for Christ might have prevented it by force of arms. *We* might be called on to bear witness to the truth by the laying down of our lives. If it is God's will for so many others, why not us?"

Papias did not immediately reply. He looked up at the cloudy sky. Curtains of misty rain were blowing by. The moon was visible among the tumbling clouds like a great eye watching them as they fled, and it reminded Papias that, without doubt, there were other eyes searching for him and his companions this night. A fox, running along one bank of the river, stopped and looked at him as the boat sailed by, but he seemed more curious than malicious. The wind continued to drive them on, and the sound of the water as the boat carved a path through it was soothing. He breathed deeply.

He looked closely at Polycarp, and then slowly drew his sword from its sheath. It was longer and wider than the short Roman sword the Praetorian had used, and more ornate. The blade gleamed, cold and proud in the moonlight. Green gems shone from the hilt. Carved on the blade were Latin words, which Papias translated aloud.

"Strength to defend righteousness" he said. "My father, you know, was a maker of swords, and he forged and designed this for me, before I left home to join the legions. Of course, I could not use it in the wars, as I had to carry the Roman swords that were issued to me. But I kept it as a memorial of my father, and have often carried it, even though I am no longer a soldier. Never have I drawn it in battle, until tonight."

He sheathed it again, and turned his eyes once more to the moonlight. "I know, Polycarp, that we may well be called on to die for Christ. If so, by God's grace, I am ready. I know I cannot save all those I love, nor can I be sure I will always escape death by the skill of my sword. Indeed, my skill nearly failed me tonight. I am not a maker of revolutions, and I do not seek open war against Rome. I am not a Zealot."

He turned to Polycarp and there was a fierce light in his eyes. "But by the help of God, I will use the strength He has given me to defend the just cause of Christ, and protect those whom the might of Rome would crush. Would any shepherd do less for his flock? Did David do less, when his sheep were threatened by the bear, or the lion, or when his God was blasphemed by the giant? Would you have had David lay down his sling and bow his head to Goliath's spear?"

Polycarp looked thoughtful but made no answer. Papias glanced back at Ignatius. "I wonder what he thinks of all this?"

To their surprise, Ignatius began to speak, though his eyes remained closed. "Perhaps if you asked him, he would tell you." He popped one eye open and smiled.

"Master Ignatius," said Papias. "I hope our conversation has not disturbed you."

Ignatius sat up and looked at them. "No, I have slept well, if not quite enough. But your talk interests me."

"What do you say, sir?" asked Polycarp. "Should we not go to our deaths as Christ did: humbly, as a lamb to the slaughter? Do we not set ourselves above God when we seek to escape the death of martyrdom?"

"We escape death every day," said Ignatius, "when we choose to eat and drink, rather than starve. Life is a gift, and Death is a door that only God may lawfully open. We turn to folly and evil when we think to open that door ourselves."

"Yes," said Papias. "We set ourselves above God by seeking death when perhaps He means us to live."

"And yet," continued Ignatius, "as Christ also said, 'unless a grain of wheat falls into the earth and dies, it remains alone; but if it dies, it bears much fruit.' It has often been His will that His servants suffer, and lose their lives. Much fruit indeed, has been borne by the death of those seeds. My friends, I will confess to you that my heart harbours a hidden desire – to follow Christ even unto the death. Of course, I too want to live, to share the joy of my loved ones, to minister to the church, and to preach the Gospel to every creature. But martyrdom – in such a death I should truly begin to be a disciple."

Polycarp and Papias pondered that remark for a few moments. "Do you mean, sir," said Papias, "that those who live to a full age and die are not truly disciples of Jesus?"

Ignatius did not quickly reply. "No," he said finally. "Perhaps I glorify that death too richly, though if so, it is only because of our Lord. It may be that only the most worthy among us may lay claim to such an honor, for martyrdom is indeed an honor."

Papias glanced at his friend, knowing that, like Ignatius, Polycarp had greatly desired the honor of martyrdom. "But surely we must beware," Papias said to Ignatius, though his eyes revealed that the words were intended for Polycarp as well, "lest we may give too much glory to those who are mere servants of the Lord. We love the martyrs, but the Son of God we worship, and Him alone."

Ignatius nodded his head vigorously. "Yes, you are right. God writes the story of our lives. And we remember that some of God's choicest servants – Mary, our Lord's own mother, for example – were not granted the martyr's crown. If only a natural death awaits us, be it so, we must accept that. But if we are called on to die by the fire, or by the wild beasts, or by the sword, then we must bow in submission to His will, and wear the crown of fire He sets upon our heads. We honor these martyrs but our worship, as friend Papias reminds us, is given only to God."

"And so," said Polycarp, "we are back where we started. We all agree that God is the Lord of life and death, and that we must take comfort in this, yielding to His wisdom. But we have come no closer to understanding this – is it lawful to take the lives of those who would make martyrs of us?"

Ignatius smiled again. "No, I suppose we haven't. I am not sure I know the answer to that question. I have never been confronted with such an adventure as we encountered tonight. Had Papias been alone, perhaps he ought to have surrendered, but he had you, Polycarp, and me, to think about, and he risked his life – for it was he alone who faced the Praetorian by the river – to save ours. Was he wrong to do so? I cannot say he was, for I am a pastor, and it may be that I shall one day be called on to defend my flock against the wolves of Rome."

All three were silent for some time, listening to the music of the river. Ignatius put his hands on his companions' shoulders. "Polycarp, you were willing to go to the Colosseum in chains, to face the terror of the fire for the honor of your Lord. Papias, you were willing to give your life to save those of your friends and brothers. Both, gentlemen, are fine examples of the love of One who laid down life itself for His friends. Your own Apostle John told us what Jesus Himself said: there is no greater love than this."

Polycarp of Smyrna

Ephesus, Asia Minor, Anno Domini 100

Clement, Mark, Lydia, the catacombs, the flight from Rome with Ignatius – all this was recalled by Polycarp and Papias as they sat by the deathbed of the Apostle John. But the hour grew late and the body had to be prepared for burial. They rose, and with final farewells, set their hearts and minds to leave their great teacher behind. At the door they turned to look on John once more. Polycarp's hand went to his chest, as if feeling for something beneath his tunic. Papias caught a glimpse of gold there, shining in the candlelight.

"Papias, do you remember what John wrote about Jesus at the end of his Gospel?"

"What's that?"

"He said that Jesus had done many more deeds than he was able to record in his book. Countless great works would remain unknown to the world, remembered only by those who knew Him. He said the world could not contain the books if all Christ's deeds were written down."

Papias nodded. Polycarp's eyes fixed on the Apostle. "Even though he is Christ's servant, the same can be said of John "

They turned and left the room, shutting the door behind them.

***

Only a year after John's death, Polycarp and Papias were grieved to learn that Clement had died. He had outlived Domitian, the Tyrant who had aimed to crush the church. Then after Nerva's rule, Trajan had given the church a respite – for a while at least. Trajan considered Christians worthy of death, but did not seek them out, and he refused to accept accusations from nameless denouncers.

Polycarp and Papias continued to work, serving the churches as elders and pastors, often travelling together throughout Europe and Asia. They grew, in age and in wisdom, and were honored by Christians in many cities. They remained close friends, though they had occasional disagreements, as they had over Papias' fight with the Praetorian. Papias found a good wife and began raising a family, but Polycarp remained unmarried, labouring alone for the kingdom of Christ. Within a few years of John's death, both men were appointed bishops of the cities where they lived: Papias of Hierapolis, and Polycarp of Smyrna.

***

Smyrna, Asia Minor – Anno Domini 105

As he sat in a small room beyond the nave of Smyrna's modest but lovely church, (a building that had been, in turns, a civil courthouse and a temple to Meles, the river goddess), Polycarp wrote a letter to the brothers and sisters in Philippi. He delighted to quote the words of God to comfort and teach his fellow Christians. His writing had been abandoned some time ago, however, for he had lost himself in reading the magnificent story of Christ as recounted in Moses, the Psalms, the Prophets, and of course the writings of the Apostles. As so often happened, he found himself looking for a familiar, well-worn page. He found the passage he was looking for: a few brief sentences written by John, from the revelation given to him while in exile on Patmos. All Scripture was good and beautiful, but these words meant more to Polycarp than any others, for they were the words of Christ Himself to the church at Smyrna, Polycarp's home: And to the angel of the church in Smyrna write: 'The words of the first and the last, who died and came to life. I know your tribulation and your poverty (but you are rich) and the slander of those who say that they are Jews and are not, but are a synagogue of Satan. Do not fear what you are about to suffer. Behold, the devil is about to throw some of you into prison, that you may be tested, and for ten days you will have tribulation. Be faithful unto death, and I will give you the crown of life. He who has an ear, let him hear what the Spirit says to the churches. The one who conquers will not be hurt by the second death.'

Refreshed by these words Polycarp rubbed his hands together to get the circulation going again, before writing once more:

'I exhort you all, therefore, to yield obedience to the word of righteousness, and to exercise all patience, such as you have seen set before your eyes, not only in the case of Zosimus, and Rufus, but also in others among yourselves, and in Paul himself, and the rest of the Apostles. They have not run in vain, but in faith and righteousness, and they are now in their due place in the presence of the Lord, with whom also they suffered. For they loved not this present world, but Him who died for us, and for our sakes was raised again by God from the dead.'

His writing progressed no further than a few more words when a noise in the nave caused him to look up.

He was concerned, a little at least: arrests under Trajan were rare, but not unheard of. He rose and walked out of the room, and into the larger chamber where the believers of Smyrna gathered for worship.

The faces that met him were familiar, and more than that, friendly. Indeed, no two faces would he have rather seen in all the world. One was that of a tall, strongly built man of near middle age, wearing a long black cloak. He smiled when he saw Polycarp.

"Papias!" shouted Polycarp in surprise. He rushed forward and embraced his old friend, whom he had not seen in nearly a year and a half.

The other face was the calm, beautiful countenance of a young woman, perhaps, twenty-five years of age.

"And dear Lydia!" said Polycarp, as he grasped her hands in his, for it was indeed the brave little girl of Rome (though now a grown woman, tall and fair). Marcus, Lydia's father, had been captured and martyred only a few months after the escape with Ignatius. Lydia's mother had died giving her birth, so Papias, who had never forgotten her, returned to Rome and adopted the little girl.

Polycarp laughed with joy as they talked, while walking the short distance to Polycarp's home. There they enjoyed a good meal, and much more good talk. The church in Hierapolis had grown strong despite the persecution of earlier years, and had continued, in the time of peace, to be nurtured in the sound teaching and courageous faith of Papias and the other pastors and elders.

"There is such hunger and thirst for the word of God in Hierapolis and elsewhere. Many who have never heard or read the Scriptures have heard of Paul or Peter or John or Matthew, and their miracles. They are very eager to hear me once they learn that I knew John. 'Tell us another tale of the Apostles,' they cry, their eyes wide like those of little children, begging their father to tell them a story. And I understand their desire. John gave me a love for the Scriptures, and urged me to study, though I shall never match your learning, Polycarp. However, many books have been written about Jesus and the Apostles that bear not the mark of Divine authorship. And helpful though they may be, they are not, I believe, so profitable to me as the words of the living and abiding voice. I shall ever thank God for the words of John that yet remain in my memory, for he opened my eyes to understand Christ's teaching, and that of all the Scriptures. Now God uses me to build up his church. Persecutions come, but the church remains. And now, in a time of peace, we build on the foundation of the Apostles and Prophets.

"But we've found a new enemy, Polycarp," he continued, "The enemy of heresy: of false teaching. Now that Rome is more or less leaving us alone, some men have too much time on their hands and they use it to invent new theology."

Polycarp nodded in understanding. Such difficulties were known to all pastors. "What new ideas have reared their heads in Hierapolis?"

Papias smiled wryly. "In our city the latest teachings

try to elaborate on the heresy that the body – anything physical – is evil. They try to subdue their bodies by spiritual knowledge but it is knowledge they do not obtain from scripture, you understand. These people are trying to escape into a 'pure spiritual realm,' whatever that means."

Polycarp replied, "Did not God create the world and the body? How can God create anything evil?"

"Ah," said Papias. "But the latest lying prophets claim that the God who created the world – the God we know from the writings of Moses – was Himself evil, and is a different being altogether from our Lord Jesus."

Polycarp nearly choked on his wine. "Well," he said through a coughing fit, "I've not heard that lie before. But I suppose we will hear it in Smyrna as well. These false doctrines tend to spread like fire in a forest."

Lydia spoke, but her voice was soft with tender emotion. "My father used to tell me to watch what I say, and what I do, but most of all, watch what I believe. For, he said, what I believe has the power to shape the way I talk and live."

The two men nodded in agreement, remembering Lydia's brave father.

."Marcus was a good man," said Polycarp. "I shall never forget him."

Lydia smiled and nodded, pain in her eyes.

Polycarp was silent for a moment. "Do you know, Lydia, that the greatest desire of my heart is to be like your father, following the path he took to the presence of our Lord? He left this world with the martyr's crown upon his brow. 'Tis a noble crown your father wears, dear Lydia."

"Noble, indeed, Master Polycarp," said Lydia, "but it is a crown of fire, nonetheless."

Papias caught his friend's eye, recalling that both Polycarp and Lydia were echoing the words of Ignatius, who saw martyrdom as an honor to be desired, but saw clearly – more clearly than Polycarp, Papias thought – the bitterness and suffering of that honor.

Suddenly, a furious knocking on the door caused them

to jump in surprise. Polycarp moved quickly to the door, but not before glancing out the window to see who was there. Then he opened the door at once, and a young man of about twenty years of age burst into the room.

"Bishop Polycarp!" he gasped with eyes wild and breath short. He seemed to be on the verge of tears.

He was one of a number of orphans that had come under the care of Polycarp and the church of Smyrna. Like many of them, he had come to Christ under the strong teaching and compassionate care of the town's beloved bishop. His name was Amplias.

"Strouthion is in grave danger sir. You remember my brother don't you? I have asked you to pray for him many times."

Polycarp nodded. He remembered Strouthion, a rebellious youth and a gambler. Now the young man had found himself in trouble with a particular government official in Smyrna: a member of the *Boule*, or Senate: the ruling Council of Smyrna. The young man had happened to insult the Senator in the hearing of one of the official's friends, and the arrest of the young man soon followed. The official charge was that he had refused to pay a debt. This was a false accusation: Amplias' brother never borrowed and could have easily paid anything that was required. He was wealthy, in fact, and his money had been gained from many years of sailing the waters of the Aegean as a pirate. Amplias told the story to Polycarp, and the name of the Senator: Seudesbar.

"My brother will be thrown into prison, if he isn't killed first!" shouted Amplias in desperation.

"Killed?" said Papias. "They might throw Strouthion into prison but they can't kill him, not even under Roman law."

"But they can!" said Amplias. "The magistrate of Smyrna himself is under this man's power."

Polycarp nodded sadly. "I'm afraid it's true. And if half of what I hear is to be believed, this man is himself the sole voice of authority behind the laws in Smyrna. Oh, the records won't show that he had a man put to death, but he can make such things happen if he wishes. We must do what we may. I shall go to the house of this moneylender and talk to him, if I can."

"Bishop," said the young man. "I love my brother, but I don't want harm to come to you on our account. Is there another way, someone else who can help us? To go to this man's house would be dangerous."

"Dangerous?" said Polycarp. "Yes, Amplias, I am sure it is. You know, my young friend, that you also serve a dangerous God. To recognize such danger around you is to hear the words, *welcome to the church*. Papias, Lydia: you should remain here. I shall return as soon as I may."

"No, my friend," said Papias. "I at least will go with you, though perhaps Lydia should stay."

But Lydia was equally adamant. "By your leave, Father, I will also come. If there is any way I can help, I want to do so, even if it is only to stand by Bishop Polycarp as he faces this man."

Polycarp looked at his friends with gratitude and a little relief. "Very well. Thank you. Come my friends, let us go."

With that he picked up his cloak and left the house, Papias, Lydia, and Amplias following.

The Senator

Smyrna, Asia Minor, Anno Domini 105

Only minutes later, they arrived at the home of the powerful senator. They were admitted by a servant who led them through the house to the room where his master's chambers were situated. The front door led to a high-ceilinged passage, and from there to an enormous hall. The house was magnificently lavish, filled with beautiful paintings and statues, luxurious carpets and tapestries.

Senator Seudesbar was from a family of devout Jews. The barrier between Jew and Gentile had been cast down within the church, but many Jews rejected Jesus and His Church, resisting it wherever it appeared. Seudesbar and his family were among these. He and his father had fought in the war with Rome many years before, and had barely escaped when Titus razed Jerusalem. Seudesbar's father had moved his family from town to town, seeking a way to make a living, and to preserve some small part of their ruined life and religion. Through diligent work, he had built up a considerable business in spices, and had increased his wealth and reputation.

But Seudesbar himself, heir to a vast fortune, had not followed in the simple path of his family and faith. Instead, he used his wealth to gain power over others, eventually holding, according to popular legend, not only the reins of political power in Smyrna, but other cities as well. He was rumored to be close to Caesar himself. It was widely known that Seudesbar's father had blamed the destruction of the Temple on the Christians, and Seudesbar had inherited his natural distrust and hatred of the followers of Christ. It was to this man that Polycarp now came, to persuade him to have mercy—something Seudesbar had, perhaps, never done. Just how Polycarp would sway such a dark heart, he did not know.

The four Christians were shown in to Seudesbar's business chambers, where he was sitting, at once leafing through a fat stack of papers, and immersed in conversation with three other men. Two of these were unknown to Polycarp, but the third he recognized as the Boularkhos, or Council Chairman: the magistrate and enforcer of Smyrna's (and Rome's) laws in the town.

"Your names?" said Seudesbar, still attentive to his papers. He was dressed in long, formal, black robes, and his hair was a silver-white. There were dark circles under his dark eyes, and the beginnings of wrinkles on his face. His voice was deep and resonant, and shifted between a cold, cruel tone that froze the blood of those who heard it, and a warm, noble quality that calmed the heart and mind.

Polycarp answered his question. "I am Polycarp, and these are my friends, Papias and Lydia. And this young man——"

"I know who he is," said Seudesbar, speaking in his colder voice. "He was here earlier. He caused quite a stir, by trying to free another whelp who did not pay his debts."

He looked hard at the boy, and there was a gleam of gleeful cruelty behind his bushy brows. "His brother, as I recall, who is now safe in our own guardhouse. This young revolutionary was to be arrested as well, for causing a public disturbance, and——if memory serves——knocking down a member of your own constabulary, Master Magistrate."

The icy gaze and voice shifted to the politician sitting across the table. "Why was he not arrested, my Lord?" he said, but the delivery of these words left no doubt in anyone's mind that it was he who was in fact the lord and not the Master Magistrate.

The Magistrate was trying very hard to cover his obvious fear with a mask of indifference and superiority, but with poor success. He was sweating, laughing, and nervously coughing, sometimes all at once, and all while trying to speak with authority.

"Well, Seudesbar," he began, "I did send a couple of

my men after him, but he eluded them by some fox-trick. They are still searching, but with him here, of course, we can——"

"We can remedy your earlier blunder," said Seudesbar, his eyes returning to the papers on the table. "Seize him," he added with an almost bored tone of voice.

Two armed soldiers stepped quickly forward and grabbed Amplias before anything could be done. Papias made a move toward them, but was firmly held back by Polycarp, who now spoke in a loud voice.

"Wait!" he shouted. "Surely you will hear our business before taking this young man away?"

After a few moments of silence, Seudesbar spoke with surprising sincerity. "Of course we will hear your business, friend," he said, looking directly at Polycarp for the first time. "Indeed, I feel certain that I know it already, for I can see in your eyes that you are no law-breaker. I have travelled widely in my lifetime, and seen much. I know the minds of men. You have come to redeem this man and his brother from well-earned punishment."

Polycarp did not speak, but whether he was simply waiting to hear more, or whether he was slightly unnerved by the canny guesses of the politician, Papias could not tell. Seudesbar paused a few moments before continuing.

"Very well: we shall set him at liberty, when the debt, and the surety for his release, have been paid." Polycarp smiled wryly. He knew that such "surety" was likely to be a ridiculous amount that few could afford.

"But I also see," continued Seudesbar, "that you are doubtful of my intentions, no doubt because you have heard evil things about me."

He sighed, almost as if he were in pain, and continued. "I am harshly used among many in Smyrna. "Oppressor" they name me; "thief" is bandied about on the tongues of the ignorant. But wealth is always mocked and slandered by idle men. Am I not a Senator, a faithful lord of the Demos, the people of Smyrna? Let the tongues wag, then. Wealth is a gift of God, as is the authority of the natural lord. By

them, I may change the otherwise unchangeable. Many
worthy things have been built that would have remained
mere ideas. No miracle worker am I, but by these gifts I
can dismiss trouble and suffering with a mere word. Your
friends, for example - shall they die for their misdeeds? This
need not be so! Come, reason with me: you will not find
better help than that which I alone can offer you now."

He smiled, and there was such generous goodwill in
his countenance, such meekness and kindness, that Papias,
Lydia, and even the boy now under arrest at the word of
this man, were swayed, thinking surely they had misjudged
him on the basis of rumors and half-truths. Seudesbar
spoke again.

"Well," he said, "is it not so? Have I not judged aright?"

Several moments of silence passed before Polycarp
answered at last. As if he had been holding his breath, he
exhaled, smiled, and even laughed. "Yes," he said. "Yes, you
are right. I have indeed come to buy this boy's freedom,
and that of his brother."

Polycarp's friends were surprised, but also relieved,
though they had no idea how he could afford to do this.
Seudesbar smiled, and bowed slightly. "Rest assured," he
said, "that the God of Abraham will use the price you pay
for the good of all concerned."

"I do not doubt it," said Polycarp, "but I fear it will
prove of little worth to you, even should you accept it."

Seudesbar's eyes narrowed as he pondered that remark.
"What do you mean?"

"I mean," said the Bishop of Smyrna, "that I have no silver
or gold to offer you. In such situations, your custom is to
throw the debtor in prison. How this helps you I cannot
imagine, unless it serves to slake your lust for revenge on
the desperate."

"It does indeed," said Seudesbar, the warmth and
nobility fading, anger rising in his voice. "But it also makes
an example to others who would think of robbing me."

"Ah," said Polycarp, "from all I have heard, robbery
should not weigh too heavily on your conscience, though

undoubtedly, this is mere slander. Still, 'the just steward fears not the whispers of his enemies,' it is said. But if imprisonment, or even death, serves your purposes, then take such a price from me."

Seudesbar froze. When he spoke, his voice was slightly softer. "What are you saying, sir?"

Polycarp answered with a resolve and nobility that easily exceeded that of the other man. "I offer myself in the place of these two men. Dispose of me how you will."

Polycarp's friends had no idea he was going to do what he did. The Magistrate's mouth hung open, and the other men who sat with him seemed both shocked and embarrassed. Seudesbar resumed his seat, and, with the words, "Leave us," dismissed his colleagues, and even the guardsmen, from the room.

Several minutes passed as Seudesbar searched the face of Polycarp. No one spoke or moved. The silence went on and on, a maddening emptiness of sound. Finally, to everyone's surprise, a smile began to spread across the face of the senator. Then, he began to laugh, and he laughed until the tears fell from his eyes. Polycarp and Papias looked at one another, unsure of how to react.

But at length, his mirth began to subside, though the smile remained, and Seudesbar breathed deeply and spoke. "Master Polycarp," he said, "I do not know if you are bluffing, or mad, or even sincere, but by the Prophets, I shall take your words for honest discourse. I have not so enjoyed a conversation, short though it was, in many years. Upon my soul, sir, but you do know how to find a man's weak spot. The boy is free to go, and his brother, too."

A great shout went up from young Amplias, and Papias and Lydia embraced him, and thanked God. Seudesbar rang a bell, and a guardsman entered the room. His lord bade him go and release the boy's brother, and within minutes he returned, leading the prisoner into the room.

The man looked tired, but thankful, for he had expected to stay in prison for the rest of his life— though he had also expected that would not be such a long time. But more than anything, he looked confused, unable to grasp what was happening. This man had mocked the church, mocked Polycarp, mocked his own brother for becoming a Christian. And, though this sinner did not know it, Polycarp had often prayed for a way to minister to him. It seemed he had found it at last."

As the rescued pirate looked around at the faces of his liberators, he met the eyes of Papias. They found to their astonishment that they recognized each other. Both started to speak, but they were interrupted by Amplias, urging them to leave. "Come, Master," Amplias said to Polycarp." Let us go." Papias and Amplias' brother nodded to each other that they would speak later.

But Seudesbar stood and began walking toward them. He spoke and the steely cold voice was back. "Wait," he said. "Your master is not going anywhere."

"But," the boy began, "You said—"

"I said you and your brother may go free. But there is still the matter of the money owed to me, and your behavior earlier today. These debts must not go unpaid."

"Yes," said Polycarp, "and now, sir, you shall be better able to judge whether I was sincere or no."

"So it would seem," said Seudesbar.

"But you cannot take him!" shouted Amplias in alarm. "He has done nothing wrong!"

"If you would prefer that I exact payment from you and your brother, as originally planned, I will do so."

"No," said Polycarp, quickly, "I will go.

He spoke words of comfort and farewell to his friends, who were anxious about what might happen next. Would the senator kill their friend, or only throw him in prison? Amplias was aware that it was his brother's sin that had brought this upon Polycarp. He begged him to change his mind.

"Please, sir," he implored the bishop, "I would not have you suffer hurt on our account. Let me go instead."

"I gave my word," said Polycarp. "And I shall not be proved faithless."

The boy hung his head, fists clenched and eyes moist. He loved Polycarp dearly, and though he had prayed for his brother's freedom, this new turn of events was in some ways a harder blow.

Seudesbar returned to his chair and was silent for several minutes. Then, he beckoned for the soldier to come near, and pointed out Polycarp. "Take this brave soul to one of our cells. Keep him there for a week—no, make it a week and a half."

He turned to face Polycarp. "It was only a small debt, after all. But don't expect the accommodations to be pleasant. I know who you are, Christian. You and your kind are worthy of far worse punishment, so take this as a moment of mercy—a rare thing for me. You have entertained me today. I shall not forget it. I have truly never heard of such reckless courage—certainly not to save such wretches from well-earned punishment."

"Perhaps," said Polycarp, "the widely-travelled Seudesbar should get out more."

The Senator roared with laughter as Polycarp was led away to prison.

Engraved in the Stone

Smyrna, Asia Minor, Anno Domini 105

Polycarp sat alone in a miserable cell. Seudesbar had built a complex of prisons on his property in Smyrna. This was supposedly done as a favour to the city, though Seudesbar's true motivation was to be able to decide who was imprisoned and who was set free. He had been known to condemn men to death, but more often he had them jailed. Seudesbar realized that a broken and cowed spirit was very useful to him. Isolation and separation from loved ones tended to make men very submissive indeed.

And this, he found, could usually be accomplished in a relatively short time. A sentence of ten days, such as Polycarp received, was typical for a first-time offender, though Seudesbar had been known to keep men locked away for years. Generally, some months after the first imprisonment, a way would be found to have the unfortunate victim jailed yet again, and this would go on, until the spirit of the man was broken. Seudesbar had decided quickly enough that he would imprison Polycarp, rather than take his life for he thought that such a man would be very useful once broken. He would have enjoyed the death of a Christian, despising them as he did, but he thought that there was more to be gained by keeping Polycarp alive. Had he known Polycarp better, he would have slain him at once.

The prison experience included a daily scourging – a brief, but painful beating that took place first thing each morning. Only one meal a day was provided: usually stale bread and brackish water. Most cells had a window: too high up to be of much use. Polycarp's cell, however, had no window. Leaky roofs and unclean floors meant that there was also damp, mildew, and rats. Many woke up at night to find a snake slithering by, or a scorpion skittering across a leg. Even ten-day sentences had been known to have a permanent effect on guests of Seudesbar.

Polycarp sat in the blackness of the cell, lonely but at peace. Polycarp was aware of God's grace. He knew that it was God who was writing the story of his life – and that God would see him through this difficult chapter.

Suddenly Polycarp saw a light. The door to the cell opened, revealing the silhouettes of two figures walking into the cell. Once they were inside, Polycarp recognized one of the faces.

"Strouthion!" exclaimed Polycarp in much surprise. "Why are you here?"

The guard laughed out loud before quitting the cell. "You people are mad," he said through his laughter. "Absolutely mad."

Polycarp was too amazed at this strange turn of events to say anything for a moment. The light from the lamp diminished as the soldier disappeared up the corridor. Strouthion was the first to speak.

"Wait, sir, a moment, please." He put his head to the door listening for the soldier's return. Satisfied that he was gone, Strouthion began feeling his way along one of the walls. Polycarp could not see him, and did not know what he was about, so he was again surprised a minute or so later when he heard a harsh, grating noise, followed by a heavy thud. Suddenly he saw part of the wall give way, a little higher than eye-level, and then, all at once, moonlight streaming in through the back of the cell.

After a few moments their eyes adjusted to the new half-light. Polycarp looked at the man, who had just pushed a loose stone from the wall right above his head.

"What in the name of wonder..." said Polycarp.

Strouthion grinned. "I found it last night and planned to push it out if I had to stay here much longer. Not big enough to escape through, and even if it were, where would we go? These prisons are too well guarded. But at least it lets in a little light. You'll find it more helpful during the day, when darkness seems so much more unbearable, somehow."

"But Strouthion why are you here?" asked Polycarp. "You were set free."

The young man looked grim and thoughtful. "Yes, I was," he said. "And I thank you for that. But I couldn't rest while you were in here! I've done many bad deeds in my life, but this was a line I couldn't cross, somehow. I went back and offered to take your place. You should have seen the look on Seudesbar's face. He laughed and said 'No thanks, that dish only goes down pleasant once a day,' by which I took him to mean that he would not let you out. But he said if I was so set on staying, he didn't want to disappoint. So he calls a soldier and tells him to escort me to a cell. Seudesbar then says to the soldier 'let him stay with his saviour,' and the soldier laughed, and said he would. So he takes me along, none too gently at that, and here I am, sir."

Polycarp smiled and said it was a noble thing to do "Well then, Strouthion, shall we make the best of it? Perhaps two together can find some solace in this dreadful place? We'll find a way to spend the time. You have already repaid me well by letting in a little light, and I thank you for that."

"Yes, sir," said Strouthion. "And I know how we might spend the time, begging your pardon, sir."

"Yes?" said Polycarp, curious.

"Well, sir, I thought you might be willing to teach me from the Holy Scriptures while we're here. I know you don't have your books with you, but my brother said there's no one that knows more of the Sacred Writings (as he calls them) than you do. As he has often said that you know them by heart, I thought perhaps you could teach them to me, sir."

Polycarp's wonder was now at a peak. "I don't know all of them from memory, Strouthion, but I will certainly teach you as much as I can. But – forgive me – why?"

Strouthion smiled. "That's a fair question, sir, and not too easily answered. But the thing is that I've done some thinking this afternoon. I thought about my brother's kindness to me, and the courage he showed; the way you took my place, and then the stories of Jesus that my brother told me — when I was sober enough to listen. Then there was that other fellow with you – Papias – I know him."

"Indeed? And how do you know Papias?"

"Well, sir, I met him in Athens a couple of years ago. He had a run-in with some of the boys of my crew. It's a long story, but to put it to the point, I saw in him a skill and soldierly mettle that I'd never come across before.

Anyway, I decided, just a little while ago, that enough was enough. I've found that sins, once they're done have a habit of staying around. They don't just disappear after the act. Sometimes I think that sin is like a great rock from the mountains, that you have to carry on your back."

He sighed, old memories coming back to him. "I've led a violent life indeed, sir. But if there's a road that leads somewhere else, I'd like to take it. My brother says I'll never live long enough to do so many sins that God can't forgive them. If that's true, then I'd like to join up with you, if you take my meaning. Maybe some day, if I live better, my brother says they may even let me go into the water for the Holy Washing, sir."

Polycarp smiled again. "Your brother's theology needs a bit of work," he said. "You can, and shall, be baptized as soon as we get out of here, if you believe with all your heart. But do you, Strouthion? Do you believe in God the Father, Creator of Heaven and Earth? Do you believe Jesus is the Christ, the Son of God and our Lord? Do you believe He was with God, and was God, and came to earth? That he was conceived of the Holy Spirit, born as a child of the virgin Mary? That He gave His life for your sins on the cross, suffering under Pontius Pilate, and descended into Hell? Do you believe He rose again on the third day, and ascended into Heaven to God's right hand, and that He will return to this world as the Judge between life and death?"

Strouthion nodded, but his voice was quieter as he answered. "I do believe all that, sir. I believe it happened and will happen, just as sure as the sun rises in the morning."

Polycarp continued. "Do you believe in the Holy Spirit? In Christ's holy church, the fellowship of His people – entrusted with the mission of discipling the nations? Do you believe in the forgiveness of sins that Christ has won, and His own promise that you, and all who believe, will rise bodily from the dead to everlasting life?"

Strouthion answered that he did, though his voice was weak with emotion. Polycarp smiled then, embraced him, and sat down with him at once to begin telling the stories of Jesus once again.

***

Over the ten days of their imprisonment, Polycarp taught Strouthion almost unceasingly – save for the few hours of sleep they were able to get at night. Each morning, they endured their scourging, and each night, they ate their miserable meal. The scourging came before the sun, and the meal came after it, so no one ever discovered their secret source of light. And that light enabled them to give better attention to the training in the Scriptures that Strouthion was now receiving. Strouthion could read and write, so he began scratching out passages of Scripture on the walls of the cell with a sharp rock they had found. One of Strouthion's favorites was a passage that showed him how Christ's life and work were prophesied in the Old Testament, many hundreds of years before His birth. He scratched out the passage on one of the sidewalls of the cell, near the corner at the back:

'Oh that my words were written! Oh that they were inscribed in a book! Oh that with an iron pen and lead they were engraved in the rock forever! For I know that my redeemer lives and at the last he will stand upon the earth. And after my skin has been thus destroyed, yet in my flesh I shall see God, whom I shall see for myself, and my eyes shall behold and not another.'

"There," said Polycarp, "engraved in the rock forever. Or at least until this rickety excuse for a prison collapses. Those are the words of Job, Strouthion, spoken in the midst of great suffering, and they show that, among other things, the hope of the resurrection of the body was not unknown to the saints who lived before Christ. They also show that the promised Messiah was to be no less than God Himself, which means, of course, that the Pharisees and others had no excuse to be so surprised when Jesus claimed to be one with the Father."

Strouthion's eyes were wide with wonder. "I didn't know men could write such things. They're the most beautiful words I've ever heard, Bishop. I should like to learn them."

Strouthion, in fact, learned them almost at once. So enthralled was he by the wonderful words that he began to carve them deeper into the rock wall, working on them every night by moonlight. He worried that his work was disturbing the Bishop, but Polycarp said no, it was a good Scriptural lesson for him to do this.

"For," Polycarp told him, "through Ezekiel God says, 'I will give them one heart, and a new spirit I will put within them. I will remove the heart of stone from their flesh and give them a heart of flesh.' And, he adds, 'they shall be my people, and I will be their God.' This is God speaking through Jeremiah of the new covenant that He would make with His people: 'I will put my law within them, and I will write it on their hearts. And I will be their God, and they shall be my people.'"

"In this same way, Strouthion, God has taken away your heart of stone, and given you a heart of flesh: a soft heart, ready to be written on by the finger of God. Your hard work in the rock is a picture of how difficult it is to write on stone. But those words you are engraving will be here as long as these stone walls last. That is a reminder that God's Word, written in your heart of flesh, will last forever. You are acting out a parable, Strouthion. Keep at it."

By the end of their ten days in prison, the Holy Words were deeply engraved in Strouthion's heart, as well as in the stone.

***

"I baptize you, John Strouthion, in the name of the Father, and of the Son, and of the Holy Spirit. Praise to the Lord, our saviour, who rescues us from the danger and sickness of our sin." The Meles River, running through the city of Smyrna, was the place where Strouthion was baptized and received into the church on the Sunday after Polycarp's release from prison. Papias and Lydia had remained in Smyrna to meet the liberated heroes. All rejoiced to hear of how young Strouthion had become a follower of Jesus – especially Amplias, who was a bundle of excitement and joy, telling the story to any who would listen. There were tears in Lydia's eyes, as there always were at baptisms. She thought of the many who had been baptized over the years by Polycarp, and by Papias, and she prayed that many more might follow.

> "Lord have mercy. Christ have mercy.
> Lord have mercy."

Thus spoke the believers gathered in the church after the baptism, faithfully appealing for the grace of Christ. Strouthion, like all new believers upon their baptism, was led into the gathering of Christians so that he might join in their prayers. Lydia watched Polycarp as he sat in the cathedra, or teacher's chair, like so many other pastors and rabbis, as far back as the days when the Jewish synagogues were first built. Polycarp led the service, reading the Scriptures from an old scroll of sheepskin, and explaining their meaning through the sermon.

The church was singing together again: "Holy, Holy, Holy Lord of Sabaoth; all creation is full of His glory." As they sang, Lydia glanced at one of the elders near the front. He was over ninety years old, and his voice sounded as if it were the voice of the very hills, so ancient and noble was its tenor. This man, she knew, had seen and heard Christ as a child, and been baptized by Peter. Yet he was always the first to say that there were many men better than he who had also been baptized by great men of God. All, he would say, should be grateful for their faith, and for their baptism, no matter whose hand brought them through the water.

The service moved on and Lydia wished that it would never end. It was like a story she thought to herself. "We hear the Scriptures read to us, recounting the great deeds of our Lord, and the story is terrible and beautiful at the same time. We kneel by the manger at the birth of the Saviour, we wonder at his miracles and teaching, we mourn at the cross, we are overwhelmed with joy at the empty tomb. Perhaps our descendants will be breathless to think of Polycarp and Papias: hearers of the Apostle John, beloved of the Lord. This glorious story is told again and again for us in our worship."

Lydia's heart was grateful as she remembered the death of the Lord Jesus Christ by sharing the bread and the wine with the believers.

"Jesus took bread, and after blessing it broke it and gave it to the disciples, and said, 'Take, eat; this is my body.' And he took a cup, and when he had given thanks he gave it to them, saying, 'Drink of it, all of you, for this is my blood of the covenant, which is poured out for many for the forgiveness of sins.'"

As Polycarp read the words he followed Jesus' own example, breaking the bread with a prayer of thanksgiving, and then taking the cup, once again thanking God. The church's deacons gave bread and wine to those who had gathered, and also carried a portion to those who were absent because of sickness or for other reasons. When the Supper was ended, all who were able gave money to help those in need. Later, Polycarp, with the help of the elders and deacons, would use it to care for the sick and the poor, the orphans and the widows, the captives and the strangers among them.

Strouthion listened with grateful heart as his first worship service came to a close, and Polycarp spoke the final words of the service. "We give thanks to you, O God, for having created the world, with all things therein, for the sake of man; and for delivering us from the evil in which we live; and for utterly overthrowing the principalities and powers, through Him who suffered according to His will. Depart in peace, in the name of the Father, the Son, and the Holy Spirit, to whom be all the glory, now and for generations of generations and for ages of ages."

"Amen."

What News the Captain Brought

Smyrna, Asia Minor, Anno Domini 107

Cool winds from the west filled the sails of a small merchant ship as night recoiled and fled before the coming dawn. The captain of this vessel stood in the prow, gazing ahead through the misty morning light. Fog had filled the air for several hours, but it was beginning to clear. The Captain, who enjoyed the quiet of the early morning before the crew got to work, turned his glance from the sea ahead, and towards his ship.

It was somewhat larger than merchant vessels of the time, designed and built by the Captain himself. He had designed it to be a smaller model of the great triremes, the warships of Greece. He had wanted a sturdy, seaworthy vessel, but one that was fast and easy to move in tight situations. Though less than half the size of the triremes, the Captain's ship had the characteristic mark of the Greek warships: a huge bow with a bronze battering ram. The Captain had his shaped in the head of a great lion with piercing, red eyes. His fellow traders thought all this expense and care foolish, but the Captain had his reasons. Though he felt no need to defend his ship against her critics, the truth was, he wanted a vessel that could out manoeuvre and outfight certain other ships: the ships of the pirates.

Several of the Captain's fellow merchants had been boarded by pirates (one unlucky fellow had been hit three times), and most lived in fear of a possible attack. The Captain's ship had never been pursued, but his precaution came from the fact that he himself had once been in prison. He was a Greek, his name was Strouthion, and he had once spent ten days in prison with Polycarp of Smyrna.

Strouthion's mother had died when he was only three, and his father was a drunkard who had fallen in a well and drowned. Strouthion and his brother, Amplias, were orphaned, and had found themselves living on the streets of Athens, with nowhere to go. One night they stowed away on a ship and the next day landed in Smyrna, which would eventually became like a second home. The two brothers found very different ways to survive their difficult life. Amplias turned to the open arms of the Christian Church, but Strouthion had taken another road. Having rejected the church, and thereby left to fend for himself, he had survived by his wits, and his quick hands. He had always loved the sea, and by the time he was twelve, he was cabin boy on the most notorious pirate craft in the Aegean Sea. At the age of seventeen, he was captain of his own ship, sailing under the colors of his former commander. For the next seven years, he terrorized the waters of the Greek islands, though he was in fact, not a killer – he plundered and made himself rich on the spoil, but always felt murder distasteful and somehow beneath him. In truth, he loved his life because of the freedom of the wild waters, not because of a burning blood lust.

But Strouthion's career had taken a different course when he met a man named Papias in Athens. While roaming the streets one night, one of Strouthion's men had tried to rob Papias. To the pirate's surprise, the intended victim turned out to be a fighter, and had knocked several of his attacker's teeth out. Five or six of the pirate's friends had joined in and it looked like certain death for Papias. But Strouthion had arrived then and intervened, suggesting that the matter be settled in a fair fight: if Papias won, he kept both his life and his purse. If not, well, they had given him a chance, anyway. The strongest, best fighter of the Captain's crew was selected for the fight, and soon two swords were flashing in the moonlight. Papias had won, quickly and decisively, with no hurt at all to himself. But rather than kill the pirate, Papias had spared him, to the astonishment of all. After that, Strouthion had bought

Papias a drink and a meal, and the two had become fast friends. Papias repaid Strouthion's intervention on his behalf by telling him about the one true God: the God who had become man, and suffered death at the hands of men, only to rise again. Though he smilingly rejected this story at the time, he never forgot Papias' words, and when he found himself imprisoned with Polycarp about a year later, his resistance to Christ ended. When Polycarp baptized him, he took the name John in honor of the great Apostle who had told Papias and Polycarp this marvellous story.

And now, two years later, John Strouthion sailed the waters of the Aegean as a merchant captain on board *The Evangel*, his very own ship. Strouthion could never forsake his love of the sea and he could not cease telling the story of Jesus to anyone who would listen. As he approached the imposing gulf that led to Smyrna, the mists began to part, and he saw his destination appear on the horizon. Smyrna was his favorite anchorage. For a start there was the fine docking facilities of the deep-water port, which allowed him to unload cargo straight to dockside, rather than first off loading into smaller boats, as he often had to do in other coastal cities.

The Captain turned his eyes back to the West, straining to see. The fog was still thick and impenetrable to sight. "Too bad," thought the Captain, "for on a clear day, I would be able to see Athens from the shores of Smyrna." He always loved berthing in Smyrna, though this time he wished there were other reasons for his visit. He came, in fact, bearing bad news to Polycarp.

***

As Strouthion's men began to unload the wares, Strouthion looked around. Normally, a guard would have approached them for papers and authorization to dock, but the only sign of life in the early morning light was a heavyset soldier in a rather shabby imperial uniform, sitting on a chair against a small, ramshackle building. He was fast asleep, his head back against the wall, and his helmet pushed over his eyes. His mouth was open, and a fly was popping in and out of it as if unsure of its way. The Captain smiled. Undoubtedly this was the man they were to report to. It seemed a shame to disturb his peaceful slumber, but then, accidents were bound to happen, and if one of these crates were to land just a little too hard on the dock...

The sudden noise woke the sleeping figure who tried to raise himself, eyes still heavy with sleep. However, his weight overcame him, and he fell back against the wall, the chair sliding to the ground with him in it. He jumped up, reaching for his javelin, but his helmet fell over his eyes again. By the time he got it straight, his cloak was tangled in the chair, and he fell hard, with a deep-throated growl of indignation. He leapt up once more, grabbing his javelin, but his helmet was covering his eyes again. In his fury, he began stabbing wildly with the javelin, finally lodging it deep in the wall of the little building, the impact bouncing him backwards, so that he landed flat on his back.

The Captain and his men could not help laughing, but when a couple of minutes had passed without any movement from the soldier, they began to wonder if he had hurt himself in his frantic awakening. The Captain walked over to him and prodded him several times. The man groaned, and began trying to get up. The Captain helped him stand. The soldier straightened his helmet, smoothed out his cloak and shook his head as if to cast off the heaviness of his recent slumber. He took a deep breath, smiled in a strange sort of way, and nodded to the Captain.

"Right," he said presently, forgetting, apparently, the ordeal of a moment before. "Where were we?" He noticed the Captain for the first time. "Oh, hello there. How might we help you this fine evening?"

Captain Strouthion looked with some thought at the early morning sky, but passed up the opportunity to comment. "No need to trouble yourself, sir. My lads are just getting started unloading our ship's holds at your fine dock. Here are our papers."

The soldier, ignoring the papers, noticed, with some

surprise, the Captain's crew, hard at work. "Unloading?" He walked over to the growing pile of casks and crates, and then turned to the Captain with a look of indignation.

"What's all this, eh?"

"Olive oil, wine, and painted pottery, mostly," said the Captain.

"Now see here, sir, you can't off load here without permission. Tell these gentlemen to cease and then step this way, if you please."

The Captain tried again to offer him the papers, but the soldier apparently did not hear. Strouthion watched him a moment as he walked back towards the little building, then turned to his crew with a sigh. "Take a break, lads. Back in a moment."

In the little building, which consisted almost entirely of a few chairs, a table, several bottles of wine (empty) and what seemed to be hundreds of documents, the Roman guard sat at the table, looking through a particularly disheveled stack of papers. He looked up to see the Captain walking across the grass to join him. Strouthion, in his wilder days, had drunk his fair share of strong drink. When he became a Christian the heavy drinking left him but he still had the appearance of someone who had lived a wild, perhaps unsteady life.

"I am just sailing my little ship into your peaceful waters," was Strouthion's reply.

"Your ship?"

"Aye. There she is, right out there. Crewed by the best sailors in the Aegean, what's more."

"Indeed, sir? Well, I am a Roman citizen and one of the Emperor's legionaries. I'm in charge of checking in all vessels importing to Smyrna, and I say you can't dock here without authorization."

The Captain nodded amiably. "No arguments from me, sir. Here are my papers, and I'm sure you will find we are on your list of approved merchant ships."

The soldier accepted the papers, but set them down without looking at them, and began rifling through some of his own papers. The Captain thought he still seemed a bit dazed, and wondered if he had hit his head a little too hard a few moments before. Indeed, it wasn't long before the soldier had all the papers in a muddle, and had even lost the Captain's papers. At length he became somewhat aware of how ridiculous he looked, and began to straighten the papers with a more official air, and cleared his throat.

"Well, sir, I don't see your name here." He paused a moment. "What is your name?"

"John Strouthion, owner and Captain of *The Evangel*."

"Spell your name, please."

"J-o-h-n."

"Not that one, the other one."

The Captain obliged.

"Now, Master Strouthion," continued the Roman guard "what's your business in Smyrna?"

"We come bearing mayhem, revelry, and insurrection in our vast holds," said the Captain without blinking.

"Very well," said the soldier, beginning to write. "Mayhem, revelry, and – what?" He jumped up, fumbling for his javelin, but his helmet clanged shut over his eyes again.

Strouthion laughed. "Be at peace, good sir. All is well."

The soldier seemed disoriented. "What do you mean?"

"It was a joke, my friend."

"A – " He opened his mouth and then closed it. "Now see here, Captain Strouthion, I think you are drunk! The emperor's legions deserve respect."

Strouthion didn't know whether to laugh, be offended or to look repentant. He opted for the latter and affected a sincere look of regret. "You're absolutely right, sir. It won't happen again. If there's one thing I tell my boys it's that disrespect for the Emperor's legionaries is disrespect for the Emperor himself. Can't think what came over me."

The soldier seemed somewhat pacified. "Well," he said, "but don't let it happen again. But as you've no papers, you'll have to pull out. No docking without authorization."

The Captain's voice betrayed a slight but growing

annoyance. "I gave you my papers only a minute ago. I believe you've lost them amongst your well-organized documents there."

"Don't mock me, Strouthion. You try handling all the work I have to do, and with little or no help, either. But if you gave me your papers, I'm sure they're here somewhere." He began picking up the papers on the floor, and several minutes' search brought the missing documents to light. "Ah, I believe that's them, back here." He had spotted them behind his chair. Strouthion stood and leaned over to see, and the guard, with a quick motion, turned himself and the chair around all at once. Unfortunately, he had his javelin tucked under his arm, and as he spun around, the wooden end clipped Captain Strouthion on the side of the head, causing him to stagger backwards, momentarily stunned.

"Yes, I believe I have them, sir," said the flustered soldier, and turned back around in time to see Strouthion, trying to regain his balance, and looking, it must be said, like a man who had been drinking hard since sundown.

"What's wrong with you?" exclaimed the guard jumping up from his seat. "You are drunk, aren't you? Aren't you?"

The Captain shook his pounding head, pulling his chair back under him. "No, I swear, though on my honor, I wish I was." As he sat back down, the soldier caught a glimpse of a dark design on the Captain's forearm.

"That marking," he said in alarm. "I've seen it before, or one very like it. Now I know what you are. You're not drunk." He thought about that a moment. "Well, maybe you are. But you're also a pirate!" His eyes narrowed suspiciously. "No wonder you didn't have any papers!"

The Captain's sense of humour was gone, replaced by exasperation. That, combined with his pounding head, removed the last shred of his patience. He spoke, and his voice took on a cold, almost gleefully villainous tone. "No, good sir, I am not a pirate. I am not even drunk. I am something far worse. I am a Christian."

The soldier gasped and pointed at Strouthion as if he

were some kind of monster. Strouthion grimaced at the astonished guard and between his clenched teeth muttered, "And I think you knew I was a Christian, because you've nearly *martyred* me with your aggravating stupidity."

"A Christian!" said the soldier, a very real fear in his eyes. "I – I should have guessed. The villains of the Empire!" He jumped up and began backing away as the Captain walked right at him, almost as if he were stalking his prey, waiting for a chance to pounce.

"Aye, that we are, sir. Does that frighten you?" He took a few steps closer as the soldier continued his cautious retreat, javelin in hand. "We're everywhere!"

The Roman soldier was nearly backed to the wall, and his eyes darted this way and that, as if he expected Christians to begin pouring in from every side. All was silent for a moment. The soldier was breathing rapidly, tense and on edge. Then, with the suddenness of lightning, the Captain raised his arms and his voice, and began singing, at the top of his lungs, one of the Psalms of David.

"Arrgh!" shouted the completely startled guardsman. He jumped backwards, banging his head against a mounted wooden shelf on the wall, and then crumbled to the floor, unconscious.

Strouthion exhaled, inwardly chiding himself for giving the poor soldier such a rough time. He bent to make sure the man was not seriously injured. As he did so, the unconscious soldier breathed out into his own face, and an overpowering smell of wine assaulted the Captain's nose.

"Drunk," Strouthion said aloud to himself. "Now, that's what you call ironic."

***

"Ironic, indeed," laughed Polycarp over dinner that evening, having just heard the story of the Captain's encounter with the soldier. "And it explains much. But here – as a pastor, I am compelled to say that you were a bit rough on the old boy, though surely you were sorely provoked. I hope," he added, "that it won't cause trouble for you. He could try to turn you in, you know."

The Captain smiled as he finished his drink. "No, it turned out all right. Five minutes later, a friend of mine came in: he's a centurion and the one usually assigned to check in ships at the dock. He returned to find his office a mess, and being run by a drunk. He is also a Christian, and he told me when I checked back with him this evening - that guard never mentioned me in his report. He may have stayed silent because of how much trouble he was in. However, I'm inclined to think that second knock on the head knocked me from his memory, but I don't know. However, we finished our work, and the boys are now enjoying a much-deserved night off in lovely Smyrna."

"Good," said Polycarp, smiling as he finished his meal. Two years had passed since the men had been in prison together. Seudesbar had intended to put the two men back in prison at some point but this had never happened, for the wealthy moneylender had died a year later. However, the single sentence had been hard enough on Polycarp. To some, he had looked older and more worn when he was released: a look that never left him. But his good cheer appeared unshakeable.

"But now, my friend," he continued. "You said earlier that you had news for me. What is your message?"

Strouthion was silent for a while, as if struggling over whether to speak. The humor of his encounter with the Roman guard felt strange and awkward now that he had to bring this particular news to his friend. Finally, he looked up at Polycarp. "My message is from Antioch in Syria, brought by way of Rheus Agathopus, a friend who lives there. It's about your friend, Ignatius."

Polycarp stiffened, now expecting the worst, but looked steadily at the Captain. "What about Ignatius?"

"He's been arrested. By order of Emperor Trajan, who happened to be in Antioch when Ignatius was denounced as a Christian."

Polycarp closed his eyes, remembering the brave bishop

with whom he and Papias had escaped from Rome years before. Strouthion continued.

"They're taking him to Rome. But there's a bit of good news, at least. They're bringing him overland through Asia Minor, and there's a good chance he will be allowed to visit friends along the way. In fact, they will likely take ship from here in Smyrna. You will be able to see him again – one last time."

Polycarp looked up with pain in his eyes. "One last time?"

Strouthion sighed, but looked right into Polycarp's face as he spoke. "He's to be executed, Polycarp, as an enemy of the Empire and the cult of Caesar. They're going to kill Ignatius in Rome."

A Fearful Love

"Here is the story, Polycarp, as Ignatius himself told it to my friend from Antioch."

It was the morning after Strouthion had delivered the devastating news, and Polycarp, though shaken, sat at the breakfast table, ready to hear the full tale. He had insisted on spending the previous evening in prayer, even before he had heard the full story of the arrest. Warm sunlight streamed through an open window, but it did not cheer Polycarp. This troubled him for he felt he should be glad for Ignatius, who had longed for the martyr's crown, and would now be given the desire of his heart. But try as he might, he could feel nothing but a sick, aching sorrow for the coming loss of Ignatius. Strouthion produced a paper from his cloak and continued.

"This is his written account of what happened. *'Emperor Trajan, after victories over the Scythians and Dacians, was seized with pride, and began to believe that the only thing he needed to do to perfect his rule was to compel all in the Empire to worship the Roman gods. For Christians, of course, this is bad news, and means a renewal of persecution, as Trajan means to put to death those who will not comply. Ignatius has done everything he could to thwart the Emperor by hiding believers who have been accused, and continuing his preaching. Ignatius, of course, is well known to the Roman officials, and it was only a matter of time before he was arrested and brought before Trajan, who happened to be in Antioch at that time.*

'Ignatius stood before the Emperor.

'Who are you, wicked wretch,' Trajan said, 'who sets yourself to transgress our commands, and persuades others to do the same, so that they should miserably perish?'

"Ignatius replied, 'Do not call Theophorus[1] wicked, for all evil spirits have departed from the servants of God. But if, because I am their enemy, you mean that the demons consider me wicked, then I quite agree with you. For I have Christ the King of Heaven within me, and so I destroy all the devices of the foul spirits.'

"And who is Theophorus?' asked Trajan.

'He who has Christ within him.'

'Do you not understand,' said Trajan, beginning to grow angry, 'that we Romans have the gods in our minds and hearts, and that they will aid us as we fight against our enemies? And who are you, if not the enemy of the gods?'

'Emperor Trajan,' replied Ignatius. 'You are in error when you call demons gods. For there is but one God, who made Heaven and Earth, and the sea, and all that are in them; and there is one Lord Jesus Christ, the only begotten Son of God, whose kingdom may I enjoy.'

'Jesus Christ?' said Trajan. 'Do you mean Him who was crucified under Pontius Pilate?'

'The same,' said Ignatius, 'and He it was who crucified my sin, along with him who was the inventor of it. Christ has condemned and cast down all the deceit and malice of the devil.'

'I see,' said Trajan. 'And do you then carry within you this crucified one?'

'Ignatius' head bowed slightly, but his voice remained strong. 'By the grace of God, I do,' he replied, 'for it is written, "I will dwell in them, and walk in them."'"

Strouthion looked hard at Polycarp before continuing. "Then Trajan pronounced sentence on Ignatius. With a condescending smile on his face, he announced, 'We command that Ignatius, who affirms that he carries about within himself the one that was crucified, be bound by soldiers, and carried to the great city of Rome, there to be devoured by the beasts, for the entertainment of the people.'"

Polycarp's eyes were down. "Did Ignatius say anything in response?"

[1] Theophorus means "The Bearer of God" and was a nick-name Ignatius used for himself.

Strouthion managed a weak smile. "Yes. He cried out with joy, *'I thank you, O Lord, that You have condescended to honor me, and have made me to be bound with iron chains, like Your Apostle Paul.'* Then, as if he took delight in them, he clasped the chains about him. He knelt and prayed for the church with tears in his eyes. At that moment, he was taken away by what my friend calls 'savage and cruel soldiers', to begin his journey to Rome."

Strouthion folded the paper and put it away.

Polycarp sighed and closed his eyes. "God have mercy," he whispered in prayer. He pictured Ignatius rejoicing in his chains. "Yes," he said softly, "Ignatius would find joy in the chains that bound him, and he is right to do so, for they are often the fitting ornaments of saints, the diadems of the true elect of God and our Lord." He opened his eyes. "Thank you, friend, for bringing this news. You said he will take ship here. Do you know when he might arrive?"

Strouthion thought for a moment. "Judging by the time of the arrest, and allowing time for the message to reach me, I should say they will be here within three or four weeks, perhaps."

"Very well. We must prepare to receive him, and do what we can to comfort him. Will you be here?"

"I'm afraid not. We will be leaving the day after tomorrow. It will be several months before I can return."

Polycarp sighed. "I'm sorry you won't be able to meet him. He is a great man."

***

A month later, Ignatius arrived in Smyrna, accompanied by a contingent of ten soldiers. Word of his arrest and journey had spread, and he had been greeted at several places along the road by Christians who prayed for him and honored him with gifts. The officer in charge was inclined to stay in Smyrna for a while before setting out again, and he allowed Ignatius to remain under house arrest in the home of Polycarp. So Polycarp was granted over two months with his friend – more time than they had ever spent together before. It was a sorrowful time, yet sprinkled with moments of joy. Papias joined them from Hierapolis, and one night, the three reminisced about their escape from Rome thirteen years before.

The light of the autumn sun streamed in through the windows, giving warmth and beauty to the dull, gray room as Ignatius spoke. "God's ways are beyond our understanding at times," he said. "I was spared that night from the sword of the Praetorian guard, but God knew that I would yet be a martyr, facing the fury of the wild beasts. And this will also happen in Rome, the city where Peter and Paul gained the martyr's crown."

Polycarp stirred a little at Ignatius' words. 'Martyrdom,' he thought to himself, 'may be a crown of glory for the martyr but it is a deadly burden for those left behind.'

"You speak of martyrdom, said Papias, "as calmly as if it were a day in the marketplace. Does God truly give such grace to the martyrs? If so, why do some deny Christ for fear of the wild beasts?"

"He does give such grace," said Ignatius. "I cannot speak for those whose courage fails them before the fire, or the sword, or the lions, but in my case, God has granted me a very practical way to prepare for the beasts of Rome."

"What is that, Ignatius?" asked Polycarp, who thought he caught a passing gleam of merriment in the ancient Bishop's eyes.

"Why, he has bound me to wild beasts before ever I come to Rome. From Syria even to your very door, Polycarp, I fight with wild beasts, by land and sea, by night and by day, being bound amidst ten leopards."

Polycarp and Papias looked at each other in confusion. "We don't understand," said Polycarp, simply. Papias, however, was beginning to understand.

"Some call them soldiers," replied Ignatius, "but they are as fierce as leopards and like them in many ways for they only grow worse when they are kindly treated. No better way to understand the ways of mad beasts than a long journey with these gentlemen, eh?" He smiled at his friends, and even laughed a little. Polycarp and Papias smiled but could not bring themselves to laugh.

"And in truth," continued Ignatius, "the rough nature of these soldiers has been a blessing, for they are a preparation for what I must face in the Flavian Amphitheater.

"The kindness of the many believers – in Smyrna as much as anywhere – has strengthened me in one way, but weakened me in another. For I have come to depend on them. Think of the generous men and women who have visited me in the last few weeks – delegations from the churches in Ephesus, Magnesia, and Tralles. More are expected, and I am grateful for their comfort. But what is the result? I grow soft. Now, as I look ahead to the time when I must harden my heart to leave your blessed home, Polycarp, I know that I cannot count on such comfort again. Once we take to the sea, the gifts will cease, the kind words will be silenced, the honor will abate. All that the church has given me will be gone – all except their prayers, for which I thank God. When I take the ship for Rome, I shall be alone, my friends, save for the Spirit of Christ who is ever with me. That shall be enough, but I will grieve for the loss of my fellow believers. I feel it already: a harrowing loneliness that I've not known before."

Ignatius' friends were surprised at this admission. He saw their astonishment and smiled. "Yes, it is true. In my youthful desire for the martyr's crown I did not realize that I had this weakness. I still desire that crown but I see now that it is truly a crown of fire – there is more to endure than martyrdom. When I was taken from my home, the fierce lions were my greatest fear, and often haunted my dreams. Yet here, in the company of my dear friends, I have come to know the threat of joy and comfort. For now my heart falters, my mind wavers, and I long to remain here with you, and not to go to Rome. I even find myself praying, as did our Lord, 'if it is possible, let this cup pass from me.' Pray for me, my brothers, that I shall again be able to say, 'yet not my will, but God's be done.'"

The smile was gone, and the eyes closed, as Ignatius put his head in his hands. Polycarp and Papias laid their hands on his shoulders, and together they prayed for strength and grace as the sunshine lit the room with fiery beauty.

***

While in Smyrna, Ignatius wrote to the various churches that had sent ambassadors to greet him. He encouraged them to obey their Christian pastors, and to be on guard against the dangers of false doctrine. He also wrote to the believers in Rome, with whom he would soon meet:

"God has answered my prayers, for I shall soon obtain the privilege of seeing your most worthy faces. As a prisoner in Christ Jesus I hope to greet you, if indeed it is His will that I be thought worthy. May I now obtain grace to cling to my lot without hindrance unto the end. For this reason, I am afraid of your love, my brothers, lest it do me an injury. I ask you, then to give me no other honor than that I may give my life for Christ. I write to the churches and impress on them all, that I shall willingly die for God, and so you must not try to save me. I beg you not to show an unseasonable good will towards me. I ask you, in the name of Christ, to do this for me: let fire and the cross come, let the crowds of wild beasts come; let my flesh be torn, my body broken and shattered; and let all the dreadful torments of the devil come upon me: only let me find Jesus Christ at the end of my suffering. Allow me to become food for the wild beasts. I do not, as Peter and Paul, issue commandments unto you. They were apostles, while I am, even until now, a servant."

***

At length the time came for Ignatius to depart. A ship had been chartered to carry the soldiers and their prisoner away from Smyrna. When the day of departure arrived, Ignatius stood with Papias and Polycarp on the shore. Many words had been spoken during his stay there, but now that the moment of farewell had come, they found speech difficult. Ignatius was grim but determined. Polycarp stood still, tears streaming down his face. Even the resilient Papias had a watery gleam in his eyes. Finally, one of the soldiers informed Ignatius that they were to board at once. The Bishop of Antioch turned to his friends, and smiled, despite the sadness that weighed on him like a stone.

"Farewell, my dear friends. I can never repay all you have given me. I will write to you, if I can. We will meet again, Papias, and Polycarp. Be strengthened in the love of God, your Father in Heaven, who has compassion on His children. Find your courage in the words and deeds of Christ, the Son of God, who died for you, and rose again, and remember that we too shall rise, and see, with the eyes of our resurrected bodies, our Redeemer stand upon the earth. Take comfort in the grace of the Holy Spirit of God who is the seal of your inheritance; the promise that this is not a final farewell."

Polycarp wept, and embraced the old man. Beyond a heartfelt "farewell" and a promise of prayers, neither he nor Papias found words to say to their friend. Ignatius was led away between two soldiers. He glanced back at his friends, "Now I begin to be a disciple," he said, and was gone. Minutes later, the ship departed with Ignatius, leaving only bitter grief in his place.

***

On board ship, Ignatius was taken to the cabin where he would stay during the voyage. The door closed behind him and all light was shut out. Alone now, there was no one to come to his aid. No kind words of fellow believers to ease his burden. No gifts of encouragement to bring light to his darkness. No human touch, no laughter, no taste of food prepared by loving hands. He was helpless in the dark. Whatever the wild beasts might do to him, the torment of his martyrdom had already begun. He knelt at once and began to pray. He wept openly, for the first time since his arrest. "O Lord," he prayed, "comfort your servant, and cause me to rest in Your wisdom and Holy will."

There was a knock at the door, and a man entered, wrapped in a dark cloak and hood, and carrying a candle. He removed his hood, and looked at Ignatius with bright eyes shining in the candle fire.

"Good evening, Master Ignatius," he said. "This is a great honor for me. I am the captain of this ship, and my name is John Strouthion. Is there anything I can do for you?"

***

Months later, Polycarp was awakened late at night by a persistent knocking on the door. He arose and opened the door. A messenger pressed a parchment into his hands and left without a word. Polycarp sat down, lit a candle, and read the document. It was from Philo, Deacon of Tarsus, and Rheus Agathopus of Syria, who had joined Ignatius shortly before his arrival in Rome, and accompanied him to his death. The full story of their journey was told there, including these words:

"In Rome, we met the brethren full of fear and joy, rejoicing indeed because they were thought worthy to meet with Ignatius, but struck with fear because so eminent a man was being led to death. He instructed some to keep silence who, in their fervent zeal, were saying that they would appease the people, so that they should not demand his destruction. He begged them to show a true affection towards him, and persuaded them not to hinder him from hastening to the Lord. Then, with all the brethren kneeling beside him, he prayed to the Son of God on behalf of the churches, that the persecution would end, and that mutual love might continue among the brethren. After this, he was led with all haste into the amphitheater. Then, being immediately thrown in, according to the command of Caesar, he was cast to the wild beasts close beside the temple. His bones – all that remained of this holy man – were conveyed to Antioch, wrapped in linen."

The parchment fell from Polycarp's hands, even as he fell to his knees in fervent prayer.

The House of Marcion

Rome, Anno Domini 140

It seemed to Polycarp, as he grew older, that time began to alter in the way it affected him. In one sense, it became more important, as the passing of years brought change to his body and spirit; but in another sense, he began to notice it less, somehow. Life became predictable, if not quite ordinary. For Polycarp's days and years were filled with family, friends, and enemies, fellow believers, and those who rejected Christ. He ate and slept, ministered and wrote letters, taught the truth of God, rejoiced and mourned. Times of peace came, and were shattered by new waves of persecution. If he was ever asked, he had to stop and think awhile to remember how long he had served as bishop at Smyrna. He often thought of his friend Ignatius. Thirty-three years had passed since the Bishop of Antioch sailed to Rome.

And now, at the age of seventy-one, Polycarp and his old friend Papias, both ancient by the world's standards, found themselves in Rome again. Both looked younger than their years but life had taken its toll on them in different ways. Papias in particular had suffered the tragic death of both his wife and his adopted daughter Lydia. It had been a difficult time for him. Lydia had left behind several children, all of whom, like their mother, were valiant servants of Christ.

Together the two men stood outside a strange house in the centre of Rome. The weather was chilly, and both men were wrapped in thick cloaks. Though age had done its natural work on them, they really had not changed all that much over the years. Their hair and beards were longer and the color had changed – Papias' was a shining silver, while Polycarp's was white as snow upon the mountaintops. Polycarp's hair hung loosely upon his shoulders, while Papias' was tied behind his head, as if prepared for work or battle. Both men walked with oaken staves, and Polycarp had a thick parchment under one arm.

The house was enormous, obviously built by a man of great wealth. It had an odd look to it that neither man had encountered before. It was difficult to say exactly what was wrong with it, but it struck the eye in such a way that it almost made Papias squint, as if he were looking right at the sun. But it was not brightness that caused this reaction, for the house was dark and ominous. The walls were high, ascending up and up, and pointing to the sky in many jagged edges. The only windows were on the upper floors, as if the house were hiding something. Papias felt uneasy but decided it wasn't the darkness, or the mysteriousness of the house that was the problem; rather it was something in the very design of the building that seemed twisted.

Papias looked at his friend. Their breath was steaming out in the cold morning air but neither had made a move to knock on the door. "Well," said Papias at last, "have we come here to admire this opulent building, or to go in and speak with its builder?"

Polycarp nodded and knocked on the door. The sound echoed for some moments before silence took over again. But no sound came from within. The wind picked up and both men felt the sting of cold air on their faces. Finally, the echoes were answered by light steps within. The heavy door opened and a tall woman stood before them. Her hair was long and beautiful, and her face was lit by a lovely smile that put both men at ease – for a moment, at least.

"Polycarp and Papias," she said, nodding to both men in turn. "You are expected. Please follow me."

Papias noted that her voice was like a song but to Polycarp there seemed to be something wrong about the voice, something twisted, marred even, like the house. The woman turned and led them down a passage with a high ceiling – so high, in fact, that in the dim light it could not be seen at all. The corridor ended abruptly at the foot of a stair. No other rooms or doors had opened to the sides of the hallway: they were going, it seemed, the only way. The stair led them up in circles, and seemed to go on forever until Polycarp's head began feeling a bit light. At last, when they must have been near the highest floor, the stairs came to an end, and they found themselves in another hall, this one much wider and longer, with many doors on either side. But the woman led them past all of these to a door directly ahead, at the end of the passage. It was black, plain and unadorned, with no sign or marking upon it.

She turned and smiled again. "My Master awaits you within. There is a small parlour inside where you may remain until he is ready for you. When the inner doors open, you may go in and see him. And now, I must leave you."

"Wait," said Polycarp. "What is your name that I may thank you properly?"

"My name is unimportant, to you or me. I have a new name, the same name as the others who believe as I do."

Papias found this very odd. "And what name is that?" he asked, a bit more gruffly than he intended.

The woman turned and began walking away, but they could hear her voice, speaking softly as she departed. "I am a Marcionite," she said and was gone.

Polycarp looked at his friend and there was a hint of anger in his eyes. "They take the name of their false bishop," he said, "rather than the name of Christ, as all Christians should."

Papias nodded and they entered the parlour. Inside, a dazzling spectacle met their eyes. The room was covered with religious imagery: paintings and statues of what seemed to be gods; others of angels and bearded prophets. A prominent picture was a mosaic of a demonic looking god waving his hand over an empty, barren earth, as if he were creating it. There were even images depicting scenes from the life of Christ, though here again, it was not the Lord Christ Polycarp and Papias knew. A large, round window let in the sunlight from the eastern wall. It seemed to cast a brilliant but unnerving illumination over all the images, giving the faces a sinister and malevolent air.

"This place has the very dimensions of heresy," Papias exclaimed.

When some minutes had passed, the inner doors opened, and the two men entered – Papias with hesitation, but Polycarp with a defiant stride. The room was dimly lit, and their eyes had to adjust after the brightness of the parlour. They looked around for whoever had let them in, but saw no one.

When their eyes had focused, they saw that they were in a place as different from the room of images as possible. Plain, almost empty, not a single image to be seen: it was cold, dark, and windowless. There was little furniture, save for a table and several roughly made chairs. In one of the chairs, his head down, and so still that they had not noticed him at first, there sat a man.

He was young, probably around thirty years of age, and his garments, black and unadorned, had, nevertheless, a well-made look to them. The man was bearded, and sat with eyes closed and hands folded, as if in prayer. He was pale and gaunt, and looked as though he had not eaten for some time. At length he looked up at them and smiled.

"Papias of Hierapolis and Polycarp of Smyrna," he said, and his voice was rich, deep, and mellow. "I am Marcion of Sinope. Your reputations precede you. Your names are seldom mentioned in my hearing save in the company of words like *fearless*, *faithful*, *valiant*, and *compassionate*: friends of the downtrodden, teachers of the ignorant, stalwarts of the church. I am honored that you accepted my invitation, for when I heard you were in Rome, I could not pass up the opportunity and pleasure of meeting you."

Polycarp and Papias made no answer, but whether they were uneasy, or simply waiting to hear more from their host was impossible to tell.

"Papias, thank you for coming today. My journeys took me, several times, near your home in Hierapolis, though the chance to meet you never presented itself. Yet I have met more than one man from your church who speaks with high praise of your tireless work."

He turned his gaze to Polycarp. "Polycarp, let us not pretend there are no differences between us for we both know that there are. The Roman Church has seen fit to reject me, but you — you are not bound by the petty politics of church authority: not if half the legends I have heard are true. I am a teacher of the truth, like you, and a bishop of Christ's Church. I am Marcion and my followers are many. Will you recognize us, Polycarp? Do you know me?"

Polycarp was standing as still as a statue, and his eyes were fixed on Marcion. "Indeed I do know you," he said and his voice was cold. "You are the first-born of Satan."

Marcion's eyes betrayed no surprise, but Papias was clearly taken aback. "Polycarp..." he said in a low tone, his voice thick with shock and reproach, but Polycarp paid no heed to him.

"Let me tell you a story, Marcion," said Polycarp. "Once there was a man who loved a very great woman. Tall and fair she was, and the desire of all who love beauty, and this young man swore many oaths to her: vows of faithfulness and love, to be hers and no other's for all his life."

Marcion spoke no word, but Papias thought he could see a change coming over his face; though if so, it was well hidden, barely discernible.

"All men," continued Polycarp, his voice rising in intensity, "promise fealty to their brides, but this young man was notable for the loud voice with which he swore to her, and the many extravagant words with which he boldly vowed lifelong devotion to her alone. His sincerity cannot, perhaps, be doubted, but the sad truth is that the young man shattered every oath with a hammer of hot steel. He disgraced his young bride by his godless adultery."

Now there was a definite scarlet tinge to Marcion's face, but still he remained silent as Polycarp went on. "Hear the meaning of my parable, heretic. You are the man who swore your oaths of loyalty to the church, the Bride of Christ. You are the man who broke those vows with false doctrine. You cheated your first love. Your sin is clear:

you reject the teaching of Holy Scripture for the ravings of your depraved imagination. The Scripture declares that there is one God; you say there are many. You say that a lesser God created the world. With the help of the devil, you have, in many countries, spread blasphemy and the refusal to acknowledge the Creator of the world as God. You despise the body and the physical universe though God himself created the world and declared that it was good. You deny the true humanity of our Saviour, rejecting what the Scriptures and the Eyewitnesses teach, namely that he was both God and man with a body of flesh and blood.

"And to add to your guilt, you support your blasphemies by tearing from the Scriptures all words that contradict you - and there are many - that you might better deceive the ignorant. You pluck from the Scriptures the writings of Moses, the Psalms of David, the words of the Prophets. On your authority alone you say we need no longer heed them. Your God is false, your Christ is false, and your Scriptures are worse than false. You are a rich man, Marcion, but the only legacy you have given the church is division and heresy."

"Enough!" roared Marcion, rising from his chair, knocking it over as he did so. "No more, sir. I extend to you the hand of grace and you slap it away? I will hear no more of this. A prophet is not without honor, our Lord said, save among his own. Very well: you complain of division in the church? You speak of vows and oaths? Here is my oath: I will tear asunder your Church and cause within her a division which will last forever!"

Papias, who had watched with a sinking heart as this scene unfolded, tried to intervene. "Marcion," he began, "Be patient, I pray you —"

"No more!" shouted Marcion again. "I invited you here to listen to me, and that I might listen to you. But instead of brothers who will talk with me about the teachings of our Lord, I get a proud bishop playing the prophet."

"Hear the final words of that prophet, Marcion," said Polycarp, in a calmer voice though there was still fire in his eyes. "Repent: make straight the paths you have twisted. Bring back those you have led astray. Turn back to the God you have rejected and seek mercy there."

"I observe," said Marcion, "that the supposed mercy of this god is ill-reflected among his servants. Leave my house at once."

"As you wish," said Polycarp, turning to go immediately. Papias stood there a moment longer, wanting to say something, but found he had been stunned into silence. As he started to speak, Marcion turned quickly away and left the room through another door. Papias sighed and followed Polycarp out of the house.

A Choice of Roads

Rome, Anno Domini 140-144

"Whatever the man's heresies — and I agree they are many and terrible — there was no reason at all to tear into him the way you did." Papias was stalking back and forth in the room of the house where he and Polycarp were staying in Rome. Frustration and anger were splashed across his face, and his voice was raised to a rare level as he spoke.

Polycarp was standing by a wide window looking up at the stars and the dim light of the waning moon. He turned to his old friend and the same frustration and anger were evident on his face too. "How long, Papias," he said, "have you and I served our churches as bishops?"

Papias grunted in exasperation, the words coming out with the force of thunder. "You know as well as I do how long," he said. "Over thirty-five years."

"Over thirty-five years," repeated Polycarp. "And I live in Smyrna, the city that boasts of being the most loyal of all Roman cities. In such a place heresies spring up like grass in the summer. In thirty-five years, I have learned to deal with these false prophets. Only the burned hand learns to keep away from the fire. And in any case, my concern is for the believers of Christ who are not being taught or who are being taught lies."

"But some of the false prophets have repented," retorted Papias, "and have served the church well. Marcion never will, I fear, after your behavior today. I hate his doctrine as much as you do, Polycarp, but I love Marcion, and pray for his salvation. Save your speeches for the deceivers who use their teaching to get rich. Marcion is not one of them. He is a moral man, whatever else may be said about him, and sincere, I believe, though surely deceived. We might have persuaded him by an appeal to the Scriptures."

"Oh, Papias," said Polycarp, frustration growing by the minute. "He knows the Scriptures as well as we do, but he has rejected them. Don't be a fool."

"Perhaps I am a fool, but your words were harsh beyond measure, and lacking in mercy. To fail to speak the truth is sin, but to speak without love is also sin."

Polycarp whirled on his friend, a fierce light in his eyes. "You, who find room in your conscience to slay a man with your own sword, accuse me of sin, and of harshly treating another? What chance of repentance was there for the soldier you killed in Rome?"

Papias shook his head. "I will not revisit that old argument, not now. Some wounds are more fearful than those made by a sword."

Polycarp looked hard at Papias. "But false prophets also arose among the people, just as there will be false teachers among you, you will secretly bring in destructive heresies, even denying the Master who bought them. Accursed children! For them the gloom of utter darkness has been reserved. For it would have been better for them never to have known the way of righteousness than after knowing it to turn back from the holy commandment delivered to them. What the true proverb says has happened to them: 'The dog returns to its own vomit, and the sow, after washing herself, returns to wallow the mire.'"

Papias threw himself into a chair at the table. "Yes, Master Polycarp, I'm impressed with your knowledge of Peter's writings. Is there a point to all this, or are you merely lumping me in with Marcion now?"

"The point," said Polycarp, nearly shouting, "is that nothing I said to Marcion was as harsh as what the Apostle said of the heretics of his day."

"Oh, of course not," said Papias, "calling an ordained bishop the first-born of Satan is merely a mild scolding. But it is one thing to attack the actions and teachings of false prophets in a letter as Peter did, and another to bludgeon a man to his face! Are we not to 'speak the truth in love,' as Paul says?"

"Are we not to 'rebuke those who contradict,' as he also says?"

"Yes, of course," said Papias. "But the motive for such rebukes must always be the restoration of the erring one."

"You mistake me, Papias," declared Polycarp, "if you think I don't want Marcion to repent. If he does I shall joyfully receive him. But there is also a time for discipline, and for Marcion that time is now, lest he continue in his folly and corrupt the entire church. I will not tolerate that. If Marcion's sin were theft, or even murder, I should deal with him differently. Sin in a Christian is lamentable, but when followed by repentance, it can be an opportunity for the light of God's forgiveness to shine. But false doctrine destroys everything – it is a poison not easily removed even when the false teacher himself is healed."

Papias made no reply, but the anger still showed on his face. Polycarp paced the room, almost unable to stop the words coming from his mouth "You think yourself a bold, brave man, Papias, and there is some truth in this: you willingly put your life on the line for the sake of others. But you have always been weak when it comes to driving out false teaching. If you will remember, that is the very reason we are in Rome: to help the church decide what to do about the teachings of Marcion, Valentinus, and others. These teachings must be dealt with. What will happen if they continue spreading? Papias, think of it! Sometimes I long for the days of persecution, for then, though many died, the purity of the Truth was maintained. But now, we risk losing the Faith itself by the scourge of these blasphemers! How many will die without Christ because of Marcion? When will you stand against these deceivers as you stood against the Roman soldier by the river?"

"Your hatred of heresy does not exceed mine, Polycarp, though you rant as if it did. The philosophers love much talking, and the multitude take pleasure in strange commandments. I delight in those who teach the truth, who speak only the words given by the Lord to the faithful. I...I am pained to learn that you think otherwise."

Silence covered the room for some minutes. Papias looked at the starlit sky and remembered nights like this spent with Lydia. They had often sat beneath the stars to talk and he asked himself what Lydia would have made of all this. Papias knew that she would bid them be reconciled, and walk together in peace. But was that now possible?

Polycarp had stopped pacing near the window and now his eyes were drawn to the night sky as well. Both he and his friend were looking at the same thing, but they did not see each other. "I go to the church tomorrow," Polycarp said, "to help make an end of this heresy. Then I take the road to Smyrna. I will fight the lying teachers there as I fought Marcion today. I hope to return with a friend who can see this, and will join me in that fight." He turned and faced his friend.

Papias looked into Polycarp's eyes, and there was resolve and pain in his voice when he spoke. "Then you return alone," he said, and cast his eyes downward.

Polycarp could not speak for some moments. When he did, his voice was barely more than a whisper. "So be it," he said and left the house with no clear notion of where he was going. He walked with haste, his anger driving him on, but perhaps he would not have hurried so, if he had known how long it would be before he saw his old friend again.

Polycarp took a room at an inn in Rome, and stayed for several weeks, talking to the leaders of the church about the rising threat of heresy. But Papias left the next day, taking the road out of Rome. He chose not to remain for the Council meeting, departing instead on a missionary journey to some of the newer churches he had helped to build, and some he had come to know in his travels. Much good was accomplished on this journey, and much good was also done by the work of the bishops and pastors in Rome.

***

Four years later, Marcion was tried for heresy in Rome. Polycarp listened as evidence was presented, and as Marcion spoke in his own defense. The trial lasted some days, and it became clear that Marcion had only hardened in his beliefs since his encounter with Polycarp.

On the last day of the trial, Marcion was excommunicated, and stripped of his bishop's title. He did not seem disturbed by this; in fact he had expected it. Marcion lost nothing in terms of power and position, for his church had grown over the years and a gift that he had given to the church of two hundred thousand sesterces was returned to him when he was excommunicated.

As the heretic walked out of the room, Polycarp turned his eyes to watch him go. Polycarp's gaze met someone else, though, standing in the back of the room. It was Papias, who had also come for the trial. In the years since their meeting with Marcion, Papias had returned several times, to talk to Marcion, and to persuade him by speaking the truth in love. At first, Marcion would not even receive him, but so persistent was Papias that at length Marcion allowed him to come in again. They had several long talks, and also corresponded by letters. But Marcion was convinced he was right, and the church was wrong. He would not give in.

And now Papias stood, gazing into the eyes of Polycarp, with even more anger. He still blamed Polycarp for Marcion's fall. The bitterness had not left him. He held Polycarp's gaze for several moments, and then walked out the door. Polycarp started to get up, to go after him, but something held him back. Finally, he turned his head back to the front, to the elder who was addressing the assembly, but Polycarp heard nothing that was spoken. When the trial ended, Polycarp left the room, and left Rome. He returned to Smyrna with as heavy a heart as he had ever known.

***

The fire crackled in the grate. Hippolytus looked up suddenly. Irenaeus had stopped speaking. Hippolytus realized with surprise that the Bishop of Lyons had been recounting the story of Polycarp and Papias for over an hour.

The Easter Controversy

The fire crackled in the grate. Hippolytus looked up suddenly. Irenaeus had stopped speaking. Hippolytus realized with surprise that he bishop of Lyons had been recounting the story of Polycarp and Papias for over an hour. So enthralled had he been, so lost in tales of days gone by, that he had nearly forgotten where he was, until Irenaeus, breaking off his narrative to retrieve his fallen papers, had momentarily brought him back to the present.

"Forgive me, Hippolytus," said Irenaeus, "I do hope I am not being too long-winded."

"Not at all," said Hippolytus, smiling. "The doctrines of Christ spoken from the lips of a master teller of tales is all too rare, and not to be missed. I find great encouragement in the story, though it reminds me of…"

"Your brother and sister?"

Hippolytus nodded. He still had nightmares about that night. "Yes," he sighed. "I often think of the night when the mobs surrounded us. I was only a boy, yet I remember with dreadful clarity the evil laughter of the man with the black patch over his eye – they called him Severus – and the stone that ended my brother's life. When the soldiers took them away, I knew I would never see them again, and I didn't. Though I never doubted God's wisdom, it was hard to lose them both at once. For years I harbored secret thoughts of what I might do or say if ever I saw Severus again. But in the wisdom of God I have not set eyes on the man again."

A strange look passed over Irenaeus' face but Hippolytus did not notice it as he continued. "I have suffered no more than others, though. You speak of Ignatius, Polycarp, and Papias. Though I am not equal to these great men, I now see that I have shared in their sufferings and their story."

"Good," said Irenaeus, "You were listening. Now, back to the story. We come to a time in Polycarp's life that is very meaningful to me, the time when I became his disciple."

Irenaeus sat back down, glancing at various parchments as he spoke. "Those were happy years and nearly everything I know as a Christian I owe to Polycarp, and the stories he told me. He taught me what Jesus taught, and he showed me how a follower of Christ should live.

"To have been taught by Polycarp is a great blessing, not to be despised," he continued. "Yet some did despise it and fell into heresy. Florinus was one. He was a friend of mine, and a fellow student of Polycarp. But he was swept away by the wind of false doctrine. It is not an easy thing for a soul, under the influence of error, to be persuaded of the contrary opinion. Let the high-minded fear, and let all Christians stand without wavering against heresies. All of us must beware, lest we also are swept away.

"But I mention those days so that you will know the source of all that I have taught you, Hippolytus. What I have given you, I learned from Polycarp. Polycarp was taught by John, and John was taught by Jesus. Our story continues theirs and even His. Those whom you teach will be the heirs of a legacy that descends from the Lord Christ. That is why I tell you my part in the story."

"After I had studied with Polycarp for some years, a time came when I was privileged to journey with him. Our travels took us many places, including Rome."

He picked up a parchment and showed it to Hippolytus. "This is an early draft of a letter I sent a few years ago to Victor, the Bishop of Rome.

"You may recall that Victor summoned a council at which he spoke in favour of excommunicating the Christians in the Asian churches. There was an argument over what day to celebrate the feast of Christ's resurrection. The Eastern churches celebrated it on the day they considered to be the actual Resurrection day and this would be celebrated on whatever day of the week that fell. The Western churches, however, always observed it on a Sunday.

"But I wrote this letter to convince Victor to reconsider his harsh treatment of our brothers in Christ. I believed that this difference was not important enough to cause discord in the church.

"I could write to Victor with some knowledge of this argument as it was this very issue, among others, that led Polycarp and I, forty-eight years ago, to the home of Anicetus, who was at that time, the Roman bishop. Let me take up the tale of Polycarp once more."

Hippolytus settled back down once again as the story continued.

***

Rome, Anno Domini 154

Dusk was passing into nightfall and the hunter's moon was waxing, several days yet from full, but still bright and large overhead. On a cool, dry evening in the autumn of Polycarp's eighty-sixth year, the ancient bishop walked the paved streets of Rome as he had so many times in the past with his old friend, Papias. But fourteen winters had come and gone since he had spoken to Papias, and the grief of that parting was seldom far from Polycarp's mind. Now, he walked with a younger disciple, Irenaeus of Lyons, and he allowed the joy of Irenaeus' presence to heal some of the wounds in his heart. Never before had he taught a student so capable and eager to learn, and it brought comfort to him to pass on the story of Jesus yet again to one so able. Irenaeus carried their meager luggage, while Polycarp carried only a book: a large work written on parchment, and bound and rolled with leather.

They found their way through the crowded streets to a modest home surrounded by public baths, sprawling courtyards, great stone fountains, and richly built, extravagant dwellings. The little house seemed out of place in the midst of such grandeur. It was so shaded by looming buildings, that it was almost unnoticeable. It was the humble house of Anicetus, Bishop of Rome.

Polycarp and Irenaeus were welcomed at the door by the bishop himself. He was younger than Polycarp, though he looked to be on the threshold of old age, but his eyes were bright and young, and the smile that shone within his thick, white beard was as welcoming as any words he could possibly say. The guests introduced themselves, but Anicetus had been expecting them.

"Come in, good Master, and you, young sir. Our meal is prepared. Others from our church here in Rome will be joining us. I hope you do not mind? Excellent. Afterwards, we three shall have time to talk. Come, this way – the dining room is near the back of the house."

Surprisingly the inside of the house was as different from its outside as its outside had been from the surrounding buildings and courtyards. There were beautiful plants and flowers in a dazzling array of colors; an enormous, wooden mantle with three lions' heads carved into it; a room full of marble shelves, richly sculpted, and laden with thick, rolled manuscripts of parchment and animal skins. In every room, walls were decorated with colorful paintings: images of birds, angels, ships, a shepherd with a lamb, a large white dove. The paintings reminded Polycarp of the catacombs in Rome, though here – removed from that deathly setting – they cheered his heart and brought a smile to his face. Irenaeus decided to ask Anicetus about the beauty of his home.

"It is often a sanctuary for those with nowhere else to go," said Anicetus. "I do what I can to make it pleasant."

They sat down to the evening meal, and here again, the contrast was astonishing. Polycarp thought of the meager (though good) food he had eaten in the catacombs, and looked in awe upon the feast before him now. Soft, hot breads and a variety of cold meat and game; rabbit cooked in a stew with sage and garlic; ripe tomatoes; sweet oranges, and more fruits than young Irenaeus had ever imagined. There were at least seven different cheeses; red wines of the highest quality and the freshest of green vegetables. And, above all, the fish – herring and salted tuna, mackerel and sardines, garfish and cod – baked and pan-roasted, and stewed with delicious spices.

"Fish!" said Anicetus in a booming voice. "What better meal for a disciple of John the fisherman, eh, Polycarp?" Polycarp nodded and smiled gratefully at his host.

Irenaeus looked at Polycarp with wide eyes. "Master," he said with a doubtful tone of voice, "All this..."

Polycarp saw that Irenaeus doubted whether such a pleasant feast could be in keeping with the sacrificial life of a Christian. He smiled in reassurance. "It's all right, Irenaeus," he said. "The Scriptures speak of feasting. There is a time for fasting, and a time for eating the little that is provided. But when God spreads the table for us, we dare not refuse. He is our Father, and He delights in the pleasure we take in His gifts."

Irenaeus was quickly convinced, and at once set about eating. In between delicious mouthfuls, he noticed that even the table itself was carefully and beautifully prepared. The tablecloth and napkins were without spot or wrinkle; candles of many colors and fragrances were lit everywhere; and decorative touches of holly, ivy, and roses gave the room a festive atmosphere. He glanced to one of the high walls at something he'd seen out of the corner of his eye. It was a dark, but beautiful painting of an enormous, brilliant star against the blackness of a midnight sky, and in the middle distance, three men riding on camels out of the East.

The meal took up nearly the whole of their first two hours in the house of Anicetus. In addition to Irenaeus, and the two bishops, there were nine others: men, women, and several children from the Roman Church. Only one servant was to be seen — a young, strong-looking man whom Anicetus introduced as "the artist who painted the work of art we have just eaten." But Polycarp was convinced that the feast was not the work of one man alone. Anicetus himself seemed to take a personal pride in the meal. Polycarp was certain the bishop had had a hand in the preparations himself. When the meal and good conversation was over, the guests began to leave, until only Anicetus, Polycarp, and Irenaeus were left.

Polycarp and Anicetus went on to speak of many things: among them, the heresies of Marcion, Valentinus, and others; the possibility of further persecutions; and the differences between the western churches and the eastern churches. Of these differences, both men were aware, and the main reason for this meeting was to talk of them, and to come to peaceful resolution, if possible.

At the moment, one of the key points of contention between east and west was over the correct date on which to celebrate the feast of Christ's Resurrection. This was the most important celebration day in the church, and it was highly valued among the suffering people of God.

Polycarp and Anicetus debated the question for three quarters of an hour but in the end, neither could convince the other to change his mind. Finally, the debate seemed to be over, and there was silence for several minutes as all three considered the words that had been spoken. At length, Anicetus smiled at his guests and spoke.

"Well, at any rate, Polycarp, whoever may prove to be right, my gratitude to you knows no bounds," he said. "In the short time you have been in Rome, you have spoken so powerfully that many have been won back from the devilish heresies of Marcion and Valentinus to the true church."

"No thanks are due to me, Anicetus," said Polycarp, glad that they were able to speak of other things after their intense debate. "I simply speak the words of John and the other Apostles. The Story of Christ, handed down by those who were eyewitnesses, this is the true mover of all that has been accomplished."

"Still, my friend, God has used you in mighty ways, and you can be thankful that you have been His instrument."

Polycarp's face darkened momentarily and Anicetus saw it, though he did not understand it. "If I have indeed been His instrument, then I am grateful indeed," said Polycarp softly. "Only our God could play a good tune on such a weathered and unworthy pipe."

Anicetus nodded, and a knowing smile peered out from

behind his thick beard. "We are frail men, Polycarp and despite our learning our understanding is often darkened. That is why that I take great care when I speak of these issues that divide us."

"Thank you for that, Anicetus. We have disagreed but we understand each other. Indeed, Anicetus, I understand well your reasons for observing the feast of the Resurrection as you do. But again, I cannot yield, for I believe our reasons stronger. The only question that remains is this: what will you do? Will you seek to have our churches removed from fellowship? Or shall we go our separate ways – disagreeing but with love and an unshaken unity? What say you?"

It took Anicetus no more than a few moments of thought to reply. "I would not break the bonds of love between us, Polycarp. Not for this. Not when we are beset by so many real enemies would I seek to make another without just cause. Had you embraced true heresy – had you taught that our Lord did not rise from the dead – then you should see how Anicetus deals with his foes. But you are no enemy to me, nor I to you. Go then, my friend, and may the blessings of God go with you."

***

They remained in the house of Anicetus for a month but in the end they left sooner than they should have liked, for word reached Polycarp of yet another wave of persecution beginning in Smyrna. When they departed, Polycarp decided to take a different route home, even though it would take a little longer. They left the city from the west, chartering a small boat to journey down the Tiber River for several miles before taking to the land.

As they stood at the dock, Polycarp was silent, remembering the night when he had escaped from Rome with Ignatius and Papias from this very spot, six decades ago. Because of the tragic way that night had ended, Polycarp had thought he would never want to see this dock again; but somehow, he was drawn to leave this way, one more time.

He glanced back at the great city of Rome. He wondered if he would ever look on it again. He was eighty-five years old — how much longer could he be expected to live? And how much longer would such travels be possible to one of his age? A weight of sadness began to burden him, and a cloud of pain darkened his heart. He was struck by a deep longing to see Papias again, one last time, before he died. And death now seemed so near, somehow. He looked at his withered hands, and was amazed to think that he was still alive. How had he managed to escape martyrdom all these years, when so many of his dear friends had not?

And yet, did it matter, in the end? As long as he could remember, he had longed for the crown now worn by Ignatius, and so many others: the martyr's crown. It had become almost like a real crown to him, one he could see clearly in his mind's eye. But now, nearing what must surely be the end of his life, he realized that not all his desire for that crown had been right. His own pride was at least partly responsible for fixing his heart on the martyr's crown. And so, he let it go. It was not to be his, he thought, and why should that matter? God was writing this story, not he.

He was suddenly aware that Irenaeus had asked him a question, but he had not understood the words. With an effort, he pulled himself from his own dark thoughts and attended his young student. "Forgive me, Irenaeus," he said. "What did you say?"

Irenaeus looked to be deep in thought as well. "Ever since our first night with Anicetus, I have been wondering, Master," he said, "why you were not more firm with him. I have heard you debate with a fire and passion wonderful to behold. And I know of your stand against Marcion…"

"Do you think Anicetus is a heretic like Marcion?"

"Well…no, I suppose not."

"As I said to Anicetus, his churches and ours have good cause to remember our Lord's Resurrection as they do. But God has not revealed how or when we ought to remember that day. We must not judge one another for such things. That is one reason I dealt with Anicetus as I did."

"One reason?"

Polycarp sighed. When he spoke his speech was awkward and halting. "The other reasons is ... Papias and I ..." He trailed off and was silent. Somehow Irenaeus thought it best not to press the matter. He knew that Polycarp would tell him if ever he needed to know.

"Come, Master," said Irenaeus, softly, sensing that his teacher was burdened with old sorrows. "Let us go now." He helped Polycarp into their boat, and soon they were sailing southward down the swift river, leaving Rome in the distance. Polycarp did not look back.

Quintus and Germanicus

Smyrna, Asia Minor, Anno Domini 155

The hum of thousands of people talking at once changed into a mighty roar of anger and derision, as a man with long, dark hair was led into the stadium in Smyrna. He was led by armed soldiers until he stood before the high dais on which sat an impressive assembly of Roman politicians and prominent citizens. In the centre sat Statius Quadratus, the Roman proconsul, beside one of his most important military personnel, General Julius. Statius would decide the fate of the unfortunate prisoner. The proconsul stood and held up his arms for silence. When the restless crowd had quieted down, he spoke to the prisoner before him.

"Tell me your name, sir."

The man seemed somewhat cowed in the presence of the proconsul and the horribly large crowd. But he cleared his throat and addressed his captors, though his voice sounded as if he were trying too hard to sound brave or defiant. "I am Quintus."

The proconsul looked over some papers he had just been given. "The centurion who brought you here says that you, and two others, turned yourselves in. Is this true?"

"Yes."

"Why?"

The man said something but no one heard it.

"Speak up, man," said the proconsul.

The man tried again, but he seemed even more timid this time. "Our faith teaches us that it is a good thing to die as a martyr."

The proconsul considered that for a few moments. "You would not be the first to die so. Yet others have had to be arrested, even hunted and captured. But you gave yourself up. Does your faith teach you that those who turn themselves in shall be rewarded above the others who have died?"

Quintus looked puzzled. Though the thoughts had never formed themselves in his mind in precisely those words, it was clear as morning that this was exactly what he had been counting on. "I...I think that perhaps —"

"Come now," said the proconsul. "Surely you have given this sufficient thought to do more than stutter and mumble when called on to answer? Will you not speak plainly to us of your purpose?"

But Quintus only hung his head, and said nothing. He was visibly shaking and deathly pale. His breath was coming in short gasps and terror was evidently coming over him. What the proconsul did not know was that Quintus had actually convinced the other two prisoners to turn themselves in with him, to seek the glory of martyrdom together. But on the way into the stadium, they had been led by their guards past the cages where the wild beasts were kept: lions, leopards, and tigers: they had lunged at the prisoners as they walked past, roaring and growling in hunger. That had shaken Quintus, and now the Roman governor and the violent crowd had quite overcome him. He tried praying but found no words to say. His fellow prisoners, watching from the side of the stadium where they were being held, were shocked by Quintus' timidity, and began to grow fearful and full of doubt.

"Well, man, have you nothing to say?" The proconsul was growing impatient; yet this was the first Christian he had ever tried, and he was interested to see how the scene would play out.

***

Sitting in the crowd, near the front, with an excellent view of the proceedings, was a muscular young man, little more than twenty years of age. His hair was long and dark, rather like Quintus', and he had a black patch over his right eye, covering the empty socket that was the result of a fight two years earlier. But his good eye was watching with intense interest, and there was a growing anger evident on his face. He was, in fact, the son of Quintus, the captive defendant, and his name was Severus. His father had become a Christian several years earlier, much to Severus' shock, but Severus had waited to see what effect this new way of life would have on him. Severus had known several Christians who had been arrested and all had denied their faith when threatened with death. Severus despised cowardice above all; he himself had been a soldier in the legions and, in general, the kind of man who would stand up to anybody, ready to fight at the slightest provocation. He walked around in an almost constant state of anger, just waiting for someone to say or do anything that he might regard as a challenge. This was how he thought a man ought to behave, and he had long thought his father quite lacking in these qualities.

Now, as he watched his father quaking before the Roman proconsul, his contempt grew to hatred – both for his father and for the faith he had embraced, which Severus now began to believe was a cowardly belief. If his father – if just one of the Christians he had known – had been brave enough to fight and die for their faith, perhaps he would not think so. Though Severus did not know it, his father was aware of his son's feelings towards him, and it was largely this awareness that had caused him to try to win his son's respect with a supreme act of valour. But now, standing before the bloodthirsty Romans, with hungry animals ready to devour him, Quintus found his natural cowardice impossible to overcome. As he stood there, unable to speak, Statius Quadratus decided that enough was, after all, enough.

"Very well," he said in a loud voice. "The altar stands before you, ready for you to burn incense to the gods, and thus renounce your ill-considered vows to this Christ. Yet you remain silent? If I recall my Roman history, Pontius Pilate, governor of Judea, found that the Nazarene himself would say little or nothing in his own defense. Perhaps you seek to imitate him. Therefore, I must take your silence as a plea of guilty. Bring forth the wild beasts!" he shouted to the soldier standing beside Quintus.

"No! I beg you! Give me time to consider!" shouted Quintus in terror, falling to his knees.

"There is no more time," returned the proconsul. "Speak, or be devoured. Will you renounce Christ? Will you sacrifice to the gods? Speak now!" His last words were spoken in a thunderous shout at the hopeless prisoner.

The stadium grew silent, waiting for a reply. There were tears in the eyes of Quintus as he nodded, and said softly, "I will sacrifice." He walked forward, and the proconsul breathed a sigh of relief. As Quintus offered the prescribed sacrifice, swearing his loyalty to the gods, for a moment he thought, "I don't really mean this. I am just doing this so I can stay alive and serve Christ elsewhere." But in his heart of hearts he did not believe his own words.

Severus stormed out of the stadium, bile rising in his throat at the thought that he was the son of such a despicable man. He vowed to do everything in his power to fight and hinder the hated Christians whenever and wherever he could. Without a glance back at Quintus, he left the stadium, and Smyrna forever, deciding at once that he would no longer live within a hundred miles of his birthplace. He never saw his father again.

***

Quintus' cowardice before the Romans destroyed any courage that his two fellow prisoners may have had. They quickly denied Christ and offered the required sacrifice to the gods. Having led his companions to give themselves up, Quintus now led them in a rejection of their faith. The crowd jeered and laughed, and hissed their disapproval and disappointment that no spectacle would be forthcoming from these Christians who were not Christians. But the proconsul Statius Quadratus raised his hands and announced that there was one more prisoner to be examined. He ordered that the prisoner be brought forth, and the crowd began to buzz in anticipation.

"This prisoner, was not among those who willingly gave themselves up," he said to Julius who stood near him. "As a matter of fact, when his name was reported to me he went into hiding. Another coward to examine. One hates to see these miserable wretches cowering in fear and then renouncing their beliefs. It's just as well, I suppose, if it has the effect of making loyal Roman citizens of them. But I wouldn't recommend them for your legion." Julius laughed.

The prisoner was brought before the assembly, and stood silently before Statius Quadratus. The Roman proconsul looked him over for some moments before speaking.

"Your name, please?"

"I am called Germanicus." The man spoke clearly and loudly, and his eyes were fixed on Statius. He was at least fifty, with flecks of white in his hair and beard, and his skin was tanned with years of working outdoors.

"Well, Germanicus, your situation is, I believe, a desperate one," said the proconsul. "Hopeless, one might call it. And yet, not quite hopeless, perhaps. You have been denounced as a Christian. The policy of our noble emperor, Antoninus Pius, and his co-regent Marcus Aurelius, is to leave you atheists alone, unless you are publicly accused. But the accuser must be able to prove his charge. A very small burden of proof is imposed on you, the accused. So, in order to disprove the charge all you are required to do is to curse the name of Christ, and swear loyalty to the gods. If you will do this, you shall go free, with no further questions asked. Please note that you are the fourth so accused today, and no one has yet had to die. I should so like to keep a clean slate for the day. But it is a day of games, you know, so, if you refuse, the wild beasts – lions, leopards, tigers, and so on, lean and hungry by now – shall be your fortune. But why talk of that? Curse Christ, and go home to your family."

"I will not."

Germanicus had spoken so quickly and loudly that

the proconsul was startled. This was the first time he had judged Christians. Given the response of the three previous defendants, he thought he understood what would happen. He had readied himself to free yet another coward. But perhaps this one was making a weak stab at valour before breaking under the pressure, a way to be able to think better of himself afterwards. Very well: Statius would give the man his moment of glory. But the proconsul was certain he would yield soon enough.

"You understood clearly what I said? You wish to face certain and violent death rather than sacrifice to the gods?"

"I understood you clearly," said Germanicus. "And you have my answer. Jesus of Nazareth is my Lord and God, and He will share neither power nor glory with the false gods of Rome."

"That should be enough to appease his inner warrior," thought the Roman proconsul. Now it's time for him to surrender. "Come," he said aloud to the prisoner. "Be reasonable. Is it such a heavy price to ask you to be a good citizen and to distance yourself from the seditious and treasonous sects? To worship the Roman gods is the essence of good Roman citizenship. Offer the sacrifice: no one here wants to see you die." The crowd murmured its disagreement with this last statement but the prisoner actually laughed out loud.

"You would waste your breath asking me again?" said Germanicus with scorn in his proud voice. "And then use your next breath to insult the church of Christ as if you expected me to honor such a statement with an answer? I did not come here to bandy words with the wicked – I came here to die. Why do you delay me?" His eyes burned fierce and his arms were taut at his side.

The crowd began to shout and jeer again. Statius was stunned by the prisoner's words. Was he really expected to sentence this man to death? Statius was not a military man; he was a politician. He didn't actually believe that Christians would be stubborn enough to die for their faith. But as he looked into the eyes of Germanicus, he knew beyond doubt that this was no false bravado, but an iron determination, impenetrable to outside force. Three times he entreated him to rejoin the Roman community, which waited with open arms to receive him. He implored him to consider his family, his friends, his life itself – a priceless treasure and irreplaceable. When this last appeal failed, Statius threw up his hands in frustration. He paced back and forth on the dais, angry and very frustrated. He whirled around and faced the prisoner once again.

"One final chance, Christian," he said, his breathing heavy and laboured. "I do not want to kill you, but I will do it. Take pity upon yourself – upon your age. How shall you hope to endure the deadly jaws of the beasts? I beseech you – nay, I command you – renounce Christ and offer the sacrifice. Save yourself, you cursed fool!"

Germanicus leapt forward in what everyone on the dais took as a threatening gesture. "No!" he shouted at the bewildered governor. "I command *you* – bring forth your foul beasts, that I may know them face to face!"

Statius staggered back and nearly fell. His anger was at a peak. He hardly knew what he was doing. "The beasts!" he shouted. "The beasts! Call forth the wild beasts!"

The company of dignitaries on the dais all leaped to their feet as one. The Roman guard standing beside Germanicus had been as surprised as everyone else when the prisoner leapt forward, and was now standing frozen, wondering what to do. General Julius shouted to release the beasts, so the guard jumped into action, grabbing Germanicus by the arm to hold him back. But Germanicus had the better will to fight him. He twisted the soldier's arm behind his back, took the sword out of his hand, and brought the hilt crashing down on the Roman's skull. The soldier crumpled to the ground, senseless. Germanicus leaped onto the dais, grabbed the proconsul by the cloak and flung him onto the sand floor of the arena. Julius rushed to the governor's defense, but Germanicus had already jumped off the dais and onto the stadium ground.

At that moment, the crowd gasped. The chaos of the scene was shattered by the horrible screams and roars of the starved and tormented lions, tigers, and leopards, who rushed into the stadium. The general was about to leap into the stadium to pursue the prisoner, but thought better of it and halted. The Roman guard was still unconscious, and Statius Quadratus was on his back, conscious but stunned, as the beasts hurled themselves right toward him like the onslaught of a terrible, nightmarish army.

With a great yell, like the vengeful Furies from the old stories, Germanicus rushed headlong to meet the beasts, leaping through the air at the last moment. The crash was terrifying, and when Germanicus came down again, his sword was stuck in the throat of a great tiger. He quickly withdrew it and struck the head off a leopard as it flung itself at him. Then another leopard took him down from behind, and he flung it off him as he turned over. The screaming cat landed right on the Roman guard, who had just regained consciousness to find the real world worse than a nightmare. In moments, the great cat had ripped out his throat.

Statius Quadratus had thus far escaped harm because all the beasts (well over a dozen of them) had turned their attention to the wildly fighting Germanicus. With a great cry, "For Christ, the Lord mighty in battle!" the noble Germanicus fell, robed in the blood of his enemies, and his body was torn to pieces and devoured by the furious beasts. The proconsul, his garments spattered with the blood of Germanicus, rushed back to the dais while he had a chance, and was helped up by Julius to safety.

He sat down in his great chair, pale and shaking. Wine was brought to him at once, but he felt sick and could not drink, though he felt he needed it badly. The vast crowd, so eager for a display of violence, was momentarily stunned by the bloody scene. When at last they began speaking again, it was a murmur of anger. They did not, as might be expected, admire Germanicus for this heroic act, but despised him, and were shocked that anyone would defy the

Roman Empire in this way. Statius heard their murmuring and realized it was up to him to address the crowd. As the soldiers brought their whips to bear on the beasts, in an attempt to rein them back in, and the body of the Roman soldier who had been killed was borne away, the governor held up his hands for silence.

He looked long at the crowd before him. He was barely recovered from the shock of what had happened. But as his mind cleared, he realized that he felt pity for the fallen Christian – pity, and admiration. But he could not voice this feeling. The crowd was growing restless in their hatred for the Christians. At length he spoke to the people.

"Fellow citizens of the great Roman Empire," he said. "Today in Smyrna we have witnessed both the cowardice and the rebellion of the sect of the Christ-followers. I wish it had not come to this terrible end. But such is the way of these people. Yet I sense that you share my revulsion at what has happened. What, then, ought we to do? How shall we answer this plague within our society? What say you?"

The people began shouting – thousands of voices together, chanting a single word in a thunderous voice of cruel demand. Statius Quadratus' head was pounding and he could not make out what they were saying. He turned to General Julius and asked if he could understand them.

"They are calling for the leader of the Christians in Smyrna to be arrested."

"Indeed?" said the proconsul. "What is his name?"

"Polycarp," answered Julius. "They are calling for the death of Polycarp."

A Place No One Can Find

Near Smyrna, Asia Minor, Anno Domini 155

It was a singular thing about Polycarp that, of all his many friends in the church, most were either martyred, or lived to a robust old age, or (like Ignatius) did both. One of Polycarp's oldest friends, Captain John Strouthion, was as hale and hearty as he had been as a young man – though he was now in fact in his seventies. It had been fifty years since he had come to Polycarp with the news of the capture of Ignatius. Now he feared the same thing was about to happen to Polycarp himself. Strouthion and Irenaeus, Polycarp's bright young disciple were walking through the dark streets of Smyrna, as quietly and cautiously as they could, keeping to the shadows, avoiding being seen at all costs.

It was one week since Quintus had denied his Lord and Germanicus died a noble death. And now the legions were out, combing the city for Polycarp. Irenaeus and Captain Strouthion were heading outside the city limits, looking for a place they had been told about – a place where they might be able to hide the hunted Bishop of Smyrna. It had belonged to the grandfather of one of Smyrna's church elders, but had long stood unoccupied. "It is a place, as I have been told," Polycarp had said to the Captain, "that no one can find indeed."

They left the city, turning south to walk through tall grass and closely crowded trees that soon became the beginnings of a wood. A quarter of an hour passed, and their way began to go up, the trees bunching ever closer together. Following the directions they had been given, they presently struck a poorly made, overgrown path that they would certainly not have found if they hadn't already known where it was. The path was narrow, ancient, and difficult to follow. Several times they lost their way, but they always found it again, though not without considerable effort. The path led them deeper into the forest, always winding around and around: up and down several hills, across a crumbling stone bridge that ran across a wide stream, through more woods, even thicker this time, then across another stream, and finally, down into a narrow vale, in the middle of which sat an old farmhouse.

It was a large structure, solid-looking, but ancient, and in need of repair. The vale opened up behind it onto the acres of land that had once been farmed, but now lay empty. The fields were overgrown, so that the house was surrounded by trees and tall grasses making it completely invisible from any vantage point in the area. It was utterly unknown even to those who lived only miles away.

"Perfect." Strouthion smiled as he spoke. "A place no one can find. Come on, Irenaeus: let's take a look inside."

At that moment, a streak of lightning lit the sky and, seconds, later, thunder boomed overhead, loud and impressive. Irenaeus jumped, despite himself. Strouthion, who had lived much of his life in violent storms, laughed.

"How wonderful," said Irenaeus, as large drops of rain began to fall. "As if it isn't cold enough."

"It's only weather," said the Captain. "You need to learn to like weather. Life has a lot of it, and it's all rather beautiful, if you know what to look for. Come on." With that, he led the way inside to examine Polycarp's next hiding place.

The sky continued to thunder. The rain kept falling and they spent the next hour looking over the farmhouse, estimating how much preparation was needed to make it livable. It was to be home to perhaps six or eight, including Polycarp, and no one knew how long they would need to stay.

They moved some fallen beams and furniture that blocked one of the corridors, and eyed a large hole in the roof, gauging the time, effort, and expense of repairs. Some of the rooms were dryer than others, but on the whole, Strouthion thought the house would do very well, and they could set about improving it once they were settled in. And anyway, he knew this was a hiding place that the Romans would almost certainly never find. The trail, after all, had gone in circle after circle into the hills, on a nearly invisible path, through many obstacles. With a fresh stream nearby, and a good well in sight of the house they had no problems with water supply. They could hunt in the woods for game, and a large apple orchard cast its long arms over the very eaves of the house. Strouthion smiled again, thanking the providence of God, knowing they could search a hundred years and never find a better place.

They unloaded their packs and began making the house as home-like as they could, looking around for anything that could be of use. They found several beds that, with clean linens, would do well indeed. A closet in one of the bedchambers revealed an unexpected treasure: books, at least two dozen of them, some rare and difficult to obtain. They looked old, and the Captain reasoned that they might have been an inheritance passed down through several generations, finally resting with an heir that little appreciated their value. 'But so much the better for us,' he thought.

Finding some unused firewood, they carried it into the large, central chamber, where the fireplace was located. Beyond this, there was little else they could do. Besides, time was of the essence: Polycarp's current hiding place was another farmhouse, much nearer the city, and not nearly as well hidden. They quickly completed their work, and prepared to return to Smyrna.

As the Captain and Irenaeus stepped outside, they found themselves in a wild, watery world. Darkness had fallen, and the rains had increased while they had been inside. The little vale was already quite flooded, and the broken road now looked more like a creek than a path.

"How long were we in there?" asked Irenaeus in amazement.

"Long enough," said the Captain, glancing at the sky. "It won't let up for some time, either. I've seen it like this before."

A gigantic peal of thunder burst overhead, causing Irenaeus to jump again. "What do we do?" he asked.

"Do?" said Strouthion. "I told you, Irenaeus. It's only weather. We return to Polycarp, at once. Come along."

The journey, difficult on the way in, was now made nearly impossible by the flooding and darkness. The return took nearly twice as long as they had spent coming in. They were already quite tired, but they pushed on with a growing sense of urgency, knowing that every moment brought the Romans closer to discovering Polycarp's hiding place. Once they were out of the woods, Irenaeus began to lead the way again, nearly running through the flooded streets, for the sense of urgency had become a fearful warning in his heart – a growing certainty that they would return too late.

When they finally arrived, soaked and freezing, at the farmhouse where Polycarp had spent the last several days, Irenaeus found his fears confirmed. The house was dark and empty. The door was torn from its hinges. Inside, they found the furniture overturned, lamps shattered on the floor, and clothing and other belongings scattered everywhere. Books and parchments were thrown about and many were torn to bits.

Irenaeus turned to the Captain, panic and grief in his eyes. "We're too late. They have him."

Strouthion looked grim, but did not speak right away. He walked around the rooms, looking at the wreckage that was certainly caused by their enemies. "No, I think not," he said. "This scene has the marks of a search – not a struggle. My guess is that the soldiers did in fact find out where Polycarp was hiding, and came here to catch him. But Polycarp got wind of the danger, and escaped in time. The soldiers, upon finding their quarry fled, tore the place apart, looking for clues as to where he'd gone."

Irenaeus breathed out in relief, though he still looked doubtful. "Y-yes, that must be it. But if Polycarp escaped, where is he now? Captain?"

Strouthion did not answer.

A Night in The Phantom's Flagon

Smyrna, Asia Minor, Anno Domini 155

Minutes later, the Captain and Irenaeus were again stealing through the streets of Smyrna, Strouthion leading and the young scholar following, somewhat perplexed. Finally, he spoke up. "Captain, where are we going?"

"A little place I know of."

This answer only further confused and irritated Irenaeus. "But *where?*"

"Just a bit further. Polycarp was wise enough not to leave a message behind that might reveal where he was going – if he even knew where he was going. We might spend days looking for him. Or...we can go to *The Phantom's Flagon.*"

"What's that?"

"It's a sort of an inn."

"Sort of?"

"Aye. Or rather, it's an inn for a particular sort of wayfarer. At one time, it was a favorite haunt of mine."

Irenaeus nodded, remembering Strouthion's dark past. "You won't have been there for many years though."

"On the contrary, Irenaeus," said the Captain, "I go there a couple of times a month. I was there the week before last, so I suppose I'm about due for another visit."

"But why?"

"Well," said Strouthion, "*The Phantom's Flagon* has been the place to go for information in Smyrna for more than a hundred years. But we need news of events that will likely be completely unknown to the regulars of *The Flagon.*"

"Then why are we going there?"

Strouthion smiled. "You'll see."

They crossed the flooded streets as well as they could

— Irenaeus fell twice, and found himself completely submerged the second time. It did not improve his anxious and miserable mood. Soon they arrived at *The Phantom's Flagon*. It was a shabby, dingy little inn, and extremely ill-kept. Irenaeus did not like the look of it at all, nor of the strange, sinister-looking men and women inside. Expressionless eyes staring from hollow faces met him everywhere. *Pale faces and pale souls*, thought Irenaeus, though every now and again he caught a glimpse of bright, piercing eyes here and there.

Still, the inn was dry. The Captain managed to find a table right next to a roaring fire and Irenaeus was glad to be out of the cold and damp. It was a loud place too, as many inns are, with a hundred conversations going on at once. A half-drunk musician was plucking away on a stringed instrument and singing at the top of his lungs words that could barely be heard above the din, much less understood. The Captain ordered wine and food, and soon Irenaeus was feeling better. But he was still worried and uneasy, and throughout their meal, he kept glancing over his shoulder as if he expected one of the sinister regulars of the inn to be standing behind him.

And suddenly, that was exactly what did happen. Irenaeus caught a glimpse of someone out of the corner of his eye, and gave a little cry of surprise. Strouthion caught him by the arm and urged him to be silent. They both looked up to see a pale, thin woman standing behind Irenaeus. She gazed intently at both of them, but was silent for some moments before she finally spoke.

"Well, Captain."

"Well, Naomi. Good crowd tonight."

"More than usual."

"Must be lots of strangers, besides the regulars. Anyone unusual drop by?"

She did not answer that, but looked around somewhat uneasily. No one seemed to be looking their way. She dropped quickly into an empty seat beside the Captain.

"What is it you want to know, Strouthion?"

The Captain held her gaze as if trying to read her thoughts. "Why don't you tell *me* what I want to know?"

She nodded, but her eyes kept darting back to the bar, and to the front door. "You want news of Polycarp."

Irenaeus' mouth dropped open but a hard glance from the Captain kept any words from coming out. "I was sure you knew," said Strouthion. "Let us speak in whispers for a moment, Naomi. What have you heard?"

"We have known for days that he was on the run, of course," she answered. "But nothing but rumors have reached us of where he has been hiding."

The Captain frowned. "That's too bad. I was hoping for something, of course. Any little —"

"Only rumors," she repeated, "until tonight."

The Captain and Irenaeus leaned forward in their chairs. Strouthion encouraged her to continue "Yes? What happened tonight, Naomi?"

"A man came in only two hours ago. He was rather short, and hooded and cloaked, so that I could not see his face. He found me almost at once, and pressed a piece of paper into my hands. Then he turned and walked quickly out, without a word. I caught a glimpse of his face then: he looked to be no more than fifteen, Captain. Have the Christians taken to employing children as spies and couriers?"

"All must play such part as they can," said the Captain. "And I think I know who it was you met. But the paper, Naomi: may I see it? Time is against us now, and every moment counts."

She reached into a pocket, pulled out a small bit of torn parchment, and handed it to the Captain. "I thought I recognized the handwriting," she said. "But I don't know what you can make of it. I doubt it will be much help."

The Captain glanced at the fragment for only a moment, then hid it in his cloak. He took a final swallow of wine, while Irenaeus looked at him, bewildered, wondering what the parchment said. "How many?" said the Captain, speaking quickly to Naomi.

"How many?"

"Here, tonight."

"Ten," she said. "Maybe a dozen at the most. But are you thinking —"

"We must go now, Naomi," he said, rising, an unexplainable fear growing in his heart.

"Wait," she said in an insistent whisper. "Not yet. Do you not see who is here?" She nodded in the direction of the bar. Strouthion looked up to see a tall, strong-looking man in a long, red cloak. He was drinking from a large tankard of ale, and on the bar in front of him sat a bronze helmet with a red plume running down the back from top to bottom. He was a general in the Roman legions.

"Julius!" said Strouthion in a frustrated whisper.

"Julius?" said Irenaeus. "He was there when Germanicus was killed wasn't he?"

"Yes, he's an old enemy of mine," said the Captain. Turning to Naomi he muttered, "He'll recognize me. We can't leave that way. We need to go out the back door."

Naomi nodded, but it was too late. General Julius had happened to glance in their direction and his eyes grew wide as he recognized the Captain. In an instant, two swords were out, and dozens of drunken men and women were scurrying to get out of the way. Irenaeus looked quickly around. Naomi was nowhere to be seen.

The General laughed as he faced Captain Strouthion, their swords only inches apart. "Greetings, Strouthion. I thought you would have died by now, old as you are."

The Captain's eyes narrowed and a hint of a smile came to his lips. "I did die, General: in a dark prison cell, long ago. But that's another story. Now my friend and I only need to leave this fine establishment. You seem to be in our way."

"Is that a fact? Maybe that's because I *am* your way out. You're both coming with me. Alive, if you so choose. Dead, if I so choose." He laughed a cruel laugh. "When you stopped pirating you might have at least taken up with more dignified companions than the Christians. I can guess what you're doing here. Looking for the old man – excuse me, I mean the *really* old man – Polycarp. Well, you can stop looking for him, because he's been found."

Irenaeus started in shock, but the Captain remained unmoved. The General let his words sink in before continuing.

"Yes, his hiding place was discovered only hours ago. He was taken to prison, to be tried by the proconsul tomorrow. That was the plan anyway, but my boys have been feeling kind of bloodthirsty lately. A man of Polycarp's age, being taken to prison by them – truth is, I doubt he survived the trip."

Irenaeus was trembling, fighting back tears. The Captain, though steady, looked a little pale. "If what you say is true," he said, "then what do you want with us?"

"Haven't you heard?" retorted the General. "There's been a general outcry against you Christian atheists. Some of our most prominent citizens have complained to the proconsul and even the emperor himself. They want anyone known to be a Christian – especially the leaders – taken and executed. So you're coming with me, and you're to be martyrs. But why should you object to that? Isn't that what you Christians want: to die for your faith? Well, here's your chance." He took a step in Strouthion's direction.

At that moment, there was a great noise of ringing metal, and what appeared to be ten or more men all jumped up from their seats, weapons in hand, and all pointed at the surprised General Julius.

"What the – " he began, looking wildly around him.

"We can settle this now, General, if you like," said the Captain. "Only – well, I don't see your "boys" anywhere around. Perhaps you'd like to meet a few of mine? I'd be more than happy to make the introductions, and from the looks of things, they're quite anxious to know you."

Irenaeus was quite as surprised as the General. He looked around at the grim, resolute faces surrounding him. They ranged from the fairly young to the very old. Most were armed with swords, though a few were brandishing long knives, or even rough-hewn wooden staves. Strouthion fixed his eyes on his adversary. "It's your call, General."

The General knew he was badly outnumbered, but he did not back down, and his sword was still poised and ready. But finally, he began to lower his weapon, and then sheathed it. "I suppose," he said, "this need not be done here. I would truly hate to see innocent bystanders get hurt. But the matter is not concluded. I will find you, Strouthion, and soon. Just like I found Polycarp." He stared at the Captain with deep hatred then turned and left the inn.

Strouthion nodded in gratitude to the faces round the room but before any words could be said, he took Irenaeus by the arm, led him down a dark passageway, and out the back door into the furious rain. Irenaeus glanced behind him as they walked. He thought he caught a glimpse of a woman, silhouetted against the moonlight, waving farewell as they hurried away.

***

The Captain walked swiftly through the night, leading his young friend as they battled the storm and flood. Both were exhausted beyond words, which was the main reason that neither spoke as they walked. Irenaeus' head was spinning: he was hardly used to such adventures, and his sorrow over Polycarp was a crushing burden. Was Polycarp alive? If so, he would certainly be dead by tomorrow, for the bishop would never recant Christ or offer sacrifices to the gods. If only they had returned sooner! But it was too late. Polycarp was taken. Tears, mingled with rain, fell on Irenaeus' face. He did not know where they were going, nor did he care. He felt a strange impulse to return and fight the general, to face death sooner rather than later.

Hours later Irenaeus, nearly sleeping as he stumbled along, thought he recognized the way they were taking. "Captain," he said, and his speech was thick with weariness. "Where are we — ?"

"This way," said the Captain, pulling his friend aside. The rain had been slowing down for some time, and now stopped completely. The moon appeared from behind its cloudy canopy, though only thin, broken beams made their way through the nearly impenetrable cover of trees (for they were, in fact, in a wood). There was an eerie silence all around. "We're safe to talk now," said Strouthion. "We needed to cover as much ground as possible before slowing down. Are you all right?"

Irenaeus nodded, but he was far from sure. "What shall we do," he said. "Can we rescue him, do you think?"

The Captain's face was invisible in the darkness, but if Irenaeus could have seen it, he would have noted a puzzled expression. "Rescue? Who are we to rescue?"

"Why, Bishop Polycarp, of course. I take it those fellows back at the inn were Christians, of sorts. Are there many more of them around here?"

"There are quite a few of them. They are an army, you might say. A secret army. They were assembled and trained by Papias, and later by Germanicus. Why do you ask?"

"Surely they are enough to storm the prisons, just long enough to free him. I don't normally hold with violence, but for Polycarp, I...I'd —"

Strouthion halted and faced his young friend. "Irenaeus, what are you...?" He stopped, as if trying to decide what he should say. Then he pulled something out of his cloak and handed it to his companion. Irenaeus tried to see it, but it was too dark. It felt like a piece of parchment. The Captain pulled him into the moonlight. Irenaeus looked again at the object in his hands. It was the paper Naomi had given the Captain at *The Phantom's Flagon*. He read the words, a single sentence: *Find me where I cannot be found.*

"Do you recognize the handwriting?" said the Captain.

Irenaeus looked hard at the writing. "I...I think I do. But how — what does it mean?"

"I told you Polycarp must have escaped. This message confirms it. He is not in prison. He sent word to the one place he knew I could be reached. Julius was just bluffing. He guessed what I had come for: the hunt for Polycarp has been on every tongue in Smyrna for days now."

Irenaeus could barely tell if he were dreaming or awake. His head was pounding. "I don't understand," he said. "What does this message mean? If Polycarp is not in prison, where is he?"

"Turn around," said the Captain. Irenaeus looked behind him, and saw that they had emerged from the wood into a little valley. A house stood before him, awash in moonlight, but also lit from within. It was the very farmhouse he and Strouthion had found and prepared earlier that day. The door of the house opened, and an old man came walking out. His hair and beard were white as snow, and there was a great smile on his face.

"Irenaeus?" said the old man. "John?"

"Polycarp!" shouted Irenaeus in a hoarse voice. He rushed forward. The two men embraced, and the Bishop laughed. But Irenaeus promptly burst into tears, and then fainted dead away.

Captain Strouthion caught him as he swooned. "He'll be all right," he said to Polycarp. "It's been a long night."

The Crown of Fire

Near Smyrna, Asia Minor, Anno Domini 155

"What will happen to the Christians who stood up for us at the inn?" Irenaeus mumbled as he tucked into a rather late breakfast of venison and eggs.

It was the morning after their adventure at *The Phantom's Flagon*. He felt better after a restful night's sleep, and everyone was in good spirits now that they were all safe in the well-hidden farmhouse.

It was a clear, winter's morning, the weather even colder than usual. At the moment, only the three of them were present in the makeshift dining room. Two believers from the church in Smyrna, and a church elder, along with two of his servants, had helped Polycarp on the journey to the farmhouse, but they had returned to their families after the Captain and Irenaeus had arrived early in the morning. One of the servants, a young man named James, had remained, in case additional help was needed, but he too would soon be returning to the city.

Strouthion finished a bite of food before answering. "No harm will come to them because of what happened last night. Julius will probably never see them again. There are many of them all over the city, and they frequent places like *The Flagon*."

"But why?" said Irenaeus.

"Because such places are often used as landmarks, and channels of information for the church during hard times," answered the Captain. "The Romans know this, and keep a close watch. Years ago, when Papias, and Germanicus, began organizing the defense of the Christians, they arranged to have regular watches kept on the churches, and on places like *The Flagon*. The watches are rotated – the men who came to our aid will not return to The Flagon for many

137

months, especially after a confrontation with a Roman general. And the Romans use such places as we do, so they have no interest in shutting them down."

Irenaeus was not so confident. "But Christians are in greater danger now, if what the General said is true."

Polycarp's interest was stirred by this comment. "What do you mean?"

Strouthion explained, "Julius said that all Christians are being hunted now, and not just the leaders. They still want Polycarp above all, but evidently they are widening the net, hoping to catch the smaller fish as well."

A look of deep distress seized Polycarp's face, and he put his hand over his eyes, but said nothing.

Strouthion noticed it and quickly added something he had already been thinking. "But he may have been bluffing, after all. I mean, if it's true, it's the first I've heard of it, and Julius is not above lying to gain an advantage. He certainly lied about having arrested you."

Polycarp's voice was weak and tired as he spoke. "But we cannot afford to take that chance. We must send word, and quickly, to everyone."

"Already taken care of, Bishop," said the Captain. "About a dozen of our men were at *The Flagon* last night and heard Julius' warning. The word will have already spread throughout the church."

"Good. But we must leave no stone unturned. I will write a brief letter, telling all our people that the time has come again to go into hiding." He paused, the weight of the news burdening him like a stone. "O Lord," he said in a voice that was little more than a whisper, "for what times have you reserved us, that we should endure these things? It never ends. Lord God, will it ever end?"

The Captain and Irenaeus looked grim but could think of nothing to say. But soon enough, Polycarp seemed to regain his strength. "Yes," he said after a few moments, "I will write a letter. James is to depart soon; I think I shall send the letter with him, and ask him to carry it to our elders. They will know what to do."

***

In about half an hour, James was ready to go. He was a servant of Phillip, one of the church elders in Smyrna, and about fifteen years old. He wore a dark cloak and a hood, and there was a gold earring in his left ear.

Polycarp walked up to him and handed him the letter to the elders. "Godspeed, faithful *doulos*," said Polycarp. "I don't know what we would do without you. Carry this message to Phillip, your master. He will know how to proceed. Take care of yourself."

"I will, sir. Thank you."

The Captain came up then, followed by Irenaeus. "I should say that's not the first letter from Polycarp you've delivered in the last day or so. Am I right?" asked Strouthion, smiling. He removed something from an inside pocket of his cloak, and handed it to James. The servant looked at the little piece of parchment and read the words, "Find me where I cannot be found."

James nodded and smiled. "Yes, I heard you got this. I must say I had my doubts, but Bishop Polycarp was sure you'd know where to go. Seems he was right. Farewell, gentlemen."

He set off at a brisk pace, and the others returned inside. James trudged manfully through the still drenched and muddy forest, following the winding pathway out of the woods, then through the grassy fields outside of Smyrna. When he was near the city, he rested in a grove of trees, remaining hidden while he pondered the best route to Phillip. Soon, his mind made up, he was on his way again.

Phillip's house was in the centre of the city, not far from the library and the *Homereium*, a shrine to the legendary Greek poet, Homer, whom many locals believed had been born in Smyrna. James chose his way carefully, taking alleys and small side streets, rather than the more widely travelled main roads. As he turned a corner into a little alley between two large public buildings, he froze. Was that a shadow he had seen, just behind him? It was gone now, whatever it was, and James breathed a sigh of relief. He moved on, even more carefully now, glancing quickly from left to right, watching for any sign of pursuers.

Soon, his master's house was in sight, and he swiftly moved to a side entrance and walked inside. The house was quiet: very quiet, for the time of day. The instant he stepped inside, James was overwhelmed by a sense of fear and foreboding. Something was wrong. Was that voices he heard, somewhere in the house? A sound behind him made him whirl around. The door he had just come through was opening, slowly – someone was coming in. He walked quickly to the end of the hall, and stole a glance around the corner into the great parlour of the house.

There, in the middle of the room, he saw Phillip, his master, elder of the church of Smyrna, lying on the floor, his eyes closed, and a great gaping wound in his chest. He was dead. James thought he saw someone else on the floor in one corner, barely moving. Standing around the dead man, talking casually, as if nothing were unusual, were three Roman soldiers. One of them looked up then and saw him, and shouted. James turned around and ran back down the hall. But he had forgotten the door he'd seen opening, and he ran straight into the arms of yet another soldier, a smirking, swarthy, giant of a man who grasped him tightly with incredibly strong arms.

"No, please, don't go," said the soldier, who had been following James since soon after he had left the grove of trees, "We have so much to talk about."

***

Polycarp pushed through the bracken and brambles to find himself in a flat, dry area: a little plateau in the hills. The opposite side of the plateau ended at the bottom of a sheer face of rock that climbed up and up into the clouds, beyond sight. At the base of the cliff face was a solitary rose bush, in full bloom. It was stunningly beautiful: a perfect picture, painted in hues of bright red and green

It was a hot day, but a cool breeze blew over him, bringing comfort, and blowing the fragrance of the roses across his face. As his eyes took in the details of the bush, he noticed that the red of the roses seemed almost alive, as if it were moving. Then, he saw why: a flame had started, somewhere in one of the blossoms, giving the red color the illusion of movement. The fire spread throughout the bush before Polycarp realized what was happening. He stepped back from the flames; then he sighed for the loss of the lovely flowers. He watched the fiery spectacle for some minutes, wanting to savor the rare beauty till the last.

But the bush did not burn up. It was not consumed by the flames. Indeed, the longer Polycarp looked at it, the brighter and more striking it became, as if most of its beauty had been hidden, and only revealed for the first time by the piercing illumination of the fire. But great drops of red color, like blood, fell from the roses to the ground, and yet the roses were redder, and fuller, than they had been. Then he noticed something else: a fiery, golden crown, in the midst of the bush, with red rubies and green emeralds and many words written in an ancient language that Polycarp could not read. And the crown was burning, and burning, but, like the bush, it was not consumed.

He stared in wonder at the sight, wishing it would never end, but a great wind came down from the mountains, and nearly knocked him over with its force. When he regained his balance, he found he was in a great, open courtyard, and it was night, but the sky was lit with the light of millions of brilliant stars. At the end of the courtyard was a dark, enclosed area, with great iron doors barring the way. Suddenly, the doors swung open and an immense, ghastly light rushed out, hurting his eyes. He looked in and saw a great and terrible furnace, lit with an enormous fire. Men were rushing to add more fuel to the fire, and as they drew near, the fire killed them and consumed their flesh.

But the fire seemed alive, somehow, and Polycarp drew closer to see what made it seem so. Then, he looked into the fire, and saw men, walking through the flames, and they were not burned. Three of the men looked like himself:

sons of Adam, flesh and blood that would one day die. But the fourth was worshipful and noble, like the Son of God. And Polycarp, unable to help himself, drew still nearer, so that the heat of the fire was all around him. And he looked at the Fourth Man and behold he wore the selfsame crown of fire that had rested in the burning rose bush. The jewels were like shining stars on his brow, and the strange writing shone forth with a great light, though he still could not read it.

He started to draw closer, to worship the Fourth Man, but the heat was too great, and he was struck down. When he raised his head again, he found himself in the upper room of a large house in a great city. Many people surrounded him, and before them all stood twelve men, and they had an air of high nobility about them. Yet one of them, the youngest, looked strangely familiar to Polycarp, like a friend long missed. "Surely these men are angels," thought Polycarp to himself. "I would that they should speak to me, but doubtless I could not understand the language of Heaven."

As if in answer to his thoughts, the great Wind returned, and filled the whole house, and as Polycarp gazed on the men, there appeared what seemed to be cloven tongues of fire, twelve in all, and they rested in the air above the men. But the fire did not consume the tongues. Then the men began to speak, and Polycarp was astonished to find that he could understand them. And they spoke of things so wondrous that he thought his heart would break with the joy, but before they had finished speaking, the house suddenly crumbled away around them, and they were under the stars once more.

Then just behind the men, a great fire leapt up, and grew until it reached beyond the very stars. Polycarp saw that the fire came from the same rose bush he had seen earlier. Then from out of the flames came a man, pierced with many wounds, but he was not dead. And he was crowned with many crowns and his eyes were a flame of fire that pierced the gloom of night.

As he gazed in wonder, Polycarp saw that this was the fourth man who had walked unharmed in the furnace. Polycarp was overwhelmed before the Burning Bush, the Fourth Man, and the Tongues of Fire. He fell to his knees. Presently one of the twelve men - the youngest - came to him and lifted him up.

Then Polycarp recognized him at last. And Polycarp's joy was so great that the tears flowed from his eyes, and he could not speak. But the young man smiled and spoke to him. "Welcome, Polycarp, my disciple, and my friend."

Polycarp knew that it was John, the Apostle of the Lord that he was seeing in this glorious dream: not as Polycarp had known him in his later years, but young and strong, as Polycarp had never before seen him, as he had been when he walked with Jesus in Judea and Galilee. And one of the other men came forward and it was Peter, the Rock, and he held something in his hands. He held it up, and Polycarp could see that it was the fiery crown that had burned unconsumed in the rose bush, and rested on the head of the Fourth Man in the furnace. Now Polycarp found he could read the words on the crown, though he could never afterwards remember what he had read there.

Peter brought the crown to John, and John stepped forward, so that Polycarp understood that he meant to set it on his head. But Polycarp protested that he was unworthy.

John held up his hand for silence. "You speak the truth, O Polycarp. You are unworthy. Nevertheless, it is the will of the One who called you that you should wear this crown, and to refuse would be disobedience to your Lord. Therefore, speak no more, but to answer me: will you accept this crown of fire, this great, unmerited honor that the Lord Christ would give you?"

Then Polycarp swooned and found himself lying on a bed, a soft pillow under his head. But the pillow began to glow, and it seemed to be on fire. The fire hurt Polycarp, but he did not get up. John's question rang in his mind, like a thousand bells, pealing in the distance, the sound carried lightly on the wind.

***

Polycarp sat up, awake in the darkness, his heart pounding, his breathing rapid. He looked out his window and saw the moon and the stars as he had seen them in his dream. He sighed and bowed his head. "I will wear the crown of fire, the martyr's crown," he whispered. "I must be burned alive."

A noise startled him, and he looked up to see the door swing open. A light from the parlour showed the silhouette of a tall, muscular man in the doorway. A sword hung from his side, and he was wrapped in a great, dark cloak.

"So they have come at last," thought Polycarp to himself. "Very well: I am ready. I will wear the crown of fire."

The man in the doorway lit a lamp, filling the room with light. Polycarp looked into the face of his captor. He stared at the man, as surprised as he had ever been in his life.

"Papias!"

The One that Returned

Near Smyrna, Asia Minor, Anno Domini 155

It was indeed Papias that stood in the doorway. For a few moments, neither moved, but stared at each other, unable to speak. Papias had a look of sadness on his face. Polycarp's face, too, wore a similar look, though it was also marked by the great surprise of seeing his old friend again. Finally, Papias managed to urge his voice into speech.

"Well, Polycarp, my friend. How long has it been? Fifteen winters?"

"I don't remember," Polycarp said. "But that sounds about right. How...how are you, Papias?"

Papias started to speak but found no words. Polycarp too looked as if he was trying to decide what to say, but he gave up after a few moments. Instead, he walked slowly over to Papias, put his hand on his shoulder, and looked into his eyes. Weak smiles crept onto both their faces, and then Polycarp embraced his old friend. The smiles blossomed then into laughter. And suddenly, it was all over: the weight and sadness of the past fifteen years recoiled like heat before a rainstorm. Minutes later, they were at the table, sharing food and drink and stories. Having already greeted Papias, Irenaeus and Strouthion retired to their rooms to give the old friends time to talk. And for hours, they did talk, as if nothing had ever come between them, recalling old memories, old jokes, even old sorrows, with gladness. As the laughter died away a contented silence settled in that lasted for several minutes. Then Papias spoke again.

"I came to Smyrna, twice," he said.

Polycarp was astonished, "You did? When?"

"The first time was about three years after Marcion's trial. The second was about five years ago. I was travelling nearby the first time, but the second time I came just to see you. You were travelling yourself on both occasions and I missed you. On finding you were not in town, I left immediately, both times. I should have written to you before coming, but I couldn't, somehow."

Polycarp looked intently at his friend. "Thank you, Papias. It's good to know that." Then he laughed again. "You won't believe me, I know, but I came to Hierapolis to see you, not once or twice, but three times."

Now it was Papias' turn to be amazed as Polycarp continued. "The last two times you were also travelling but the first time, I — I am ashamed to admit that you were there, but I turned around without visiting you. What was it? Cowardice? Pride? Probably both, if I know myself at all. And I wrote several letters to you, but never sent them."

Papias nodded. "I did the same. And something I wrote in those letters needs to be said now. Polycarp…our quarrel over Marcion — "

"No," interrupted Polycarp. "You must allow me to speak first. I was wrong, and I beg you to forgive me. Not in the truth of what I said to Marcion: his heresies were and remain damnable, but…well, you were right, Papias. I could have seasoned my words with grace. In my zeal for Christ and His Church, I spoke harshly, and perhaps drove him away without need. There was pride at work in my heart then, as well. No, hear me: many years ago, Ignatius wrote to me after he left Smyrna to go to his death in Rome. I have ever treasured that letter, but I would have done well to remember his words and put them into practice.

'If you love the good disciples only,' Ignatius wrote, 'you have no grace. Rather, subdue those that are evil by gentleness. All wounds are not healed by the same medicine. Ease the pain of cutting by tenderness.'

"And there is more: my own words return to me to accuse — for I wrote to the believers in Philippi concerning Valens, an elder there who fell into grievous sin. As I exhorted them how they should deal with him, I enjoined them to not count him or those like him as enemies, but to deal with them as suffering and straying brothers, calling them back to repentance. Little did I heed my own counsel."

"We walk the road of grace, but it is a long, slow journey. At that time, it had not been granted to me to practice what is written: be angry and sin not. Many words I spoke in anger that night, and truth lay behind some, no doubt. But one thing I wish to take back, for it was simply untrue: I said then that you were weak in the fight against heresy. Your teaching and writing stand as witnesses against my words. I desire your forgiveness for that above all."

"It is yours, and gladly," said Papias. "And I am grateful for your words, Polycarp. But there is more to be said. Your approach to Marcion was too harsh; I certainly thought so. But there are times when such words must be used with someone who refuses to repent. Christ Himself spoke thus at times, as did the Apostles. Wisdom is needed to discern such moments. Was that moment in Rome the proper time to deal with Marcion? I'm not sure. But I will tell you this: I visited Marcion many times after our first visit in Rome."

"Did you indeed? I never knew that."

Papias nodded. "I learned much in our speech together, and gained a clearer picture of the man's character. He is genuinely convinced of the truth of his doctrine, but there is a subtle pride lurking in his heart, and so deeply buried that he cannot see it himself. I became convinced that his invitation to us was merely an attempt to gain our blessings on his doctrine, which of course could never happen. He likes to talk, and is a good listener, too, but he often listens only for his next opportunity to speak. I did all I could to persuade him, and we went to the Scriptures time and again. But the Scriptures will only change the mind of a man who believes them to be the Word of God, and Marcion had already rejected much of God's Word. And so, whether you or I were in the right, I do not know, but I have learned much, and I do not believe that a gentler approach by you would have won him."

"I hope you're right," Polycarp said. "Marcion's rejection of the Holy Scriptures was, I think, the one thing that angered me the most. The Word of God has been an ever present comfort to me over the years."

"Of course," said Papias, with a smile. "And do you know the one passage of Scripture that comes to my mind these days? It reminds me of you. And of myself, of course."

"What's that?"

Papias, putting his hands behind his back, stood to quote the Sacred Words, clearing his throat before speaking: "And now, behold, I am this day eighty-five years old. I am still as strong today as I was in the day that Moses sent me; my strength now is as my strength was then, for war and for going and coming. 'Tis the words of Caleb, the faithful spy of Israel." He sat back down again, with a flourish.

Polycarp laughed. "So you're saying I'm old enough to remember the days of Moses, eh?"

They both laughed together. "No," said Papias finally. "But we're both even older than Caleb now, if only a little. Yet here we are. We've even lived longer than John."

Polycarp shook his head in amazement. "I truly never thought we'd last this long."

They were both silent for a while. Then Polycarp spoke again. "You were often in my prayers."

"As were you in mine."

Polycarp sighed, but smiled. "All this distance between us, all these years – it has made me miss dear Lydia all the more. She would never have let us quarrel like that in the first place or she would have worked tirelessly to reconcile us."

Papias smiled. "Yes," he said softly, "our differences would have only lasted hours had she been with us. And yet, good came of it all. My missionary work that I began upon leaving Rome has yielded a great harvest, and the churches have flourished. And I have heard much about the tremendous work you did in Rome to combat false teaching. Many were won from the Enemy in those days."

"Yes, there is much to be grateful for. But no gift is

dearer to me than your presence here, my friend. Especially now. I..." His voice trailed off, and a shadow seemed to pass over him.

"What is it, Polycarp?"

Polycarp looked at Papias, but he was hesitant to speak. "You know of the Romans' search for me. You managed to find me, though I hide in the midst of the wilderness. That's just what I'd expect of you. But the Romans will also find me, sooner or later. Sooner, I should think, unless dreams prove to be great liars."

Papias found this remark puzzling. "They can be the worst of liars at times," he said. "What have you dreamed?"

Polycarp shook his head. "I will tell you, Papias," he said, "but not tonight. For what's left of the night let us rest awhile. Tomorrow, we will take counsel together, and I will tell you all." He smiled at Papias. "It's wonderful to see you again, my old companion. The joy of this reunion, we owe to God, and to you."

"No, Polycarp. To God alone. But we may also thank each other, for we both set aside our pride, and our differences, to be together again."

"Yes, we did," said Polycarp. "But you were the one that returned."

***

The next three days were perhaps the best of Polycarp's long life. All fear of danger was forgotten, as he and Papias, and their friends Strouthion and Irenaeus, laughed and talked, and read the Scriptures or other favorite books. Papias and the Strouthion enjoyed Homer and Aeschylus, while Polycarp and Irenaeus preferred Aristotle or the histories of Josephus. They also prayed, worked, and enjoyed meals together. The dark days of persecution were so distant that they seemed almost unreal.

Just after sunset on the third day after Papias' arrival, Strouthion was taking a walk after dinner. He didn't mind the cold weather as much as the others, and enjoyed being alone outside to think and to pray. As he strolled along the edges of the wood, he stopped, suddenly, for he had heard a noise: faint, but growing louder, as if someone were walking towards him out of the darkness. He crouched behind a tree, his hand on his sword hilt, and waited.

Presently the source of the sound came in view. It was a young man, in a torn cloak. His face was caked with dried blood, and fresh blood was trickling from an open wound on the side of his head. He was staggering along, limping, and holding his arm as if it were injured. Strouthion recognized him as Stephen, another servant of Phillip, the church elder. Strouthion rushed over to him, and caught him as he stumbled on a tree root.

"Stephen! What has happened, lad?"

The young man seemed disoriented and it was some moments before he could focus on who had spoken to him. "C-Captain?"

"Yes, it's me. What has happened?"

"Take me to Polycarp. The Romans are coming. We are betrayed." He fainted, and was carried quickly inside.

***

The young man named Stephen was badly injured: in addition to a nasty knock on his head, and many bruises, his arm was broken, and his ankle was sprained. The Captain remarked that he looked as if he had been thrown several times against a stone wall. As a matter of fact, that was just about what had happened to him.

"It's a miracle he made it here," said Polycarp. "We must let him rest."

"We have to talk to him," said the Captain. "He said the Romans are coming. We must know what he knows. Stephen," said Strouthion. "I know you're in a lot of pain, but you must speak to us, if you can. All right?"

Stephen nodded. The others crowded around, anxious to hear.

"Good," said the Captain. "Now, you said that the Romans are coming; that we were betrayed. Betrayed by whom?"

"By...by James."

Polycarp and Strouthion looked at each other in shock. It was not possible that Phillip's faithful servant had betrayed them. Stephen seemed to understand their thoughts, and spoke up again. "Not...willingly. They tortured him ... M-mercilessly...over several days. I watched the whole thing. He was feverish and delirious. I am sure he never realized he had told them anything."

Stephen told them how the Romans had sought out Phillip, knowing him to be one of the church's elders. They had found him at home, just as he and Stephen were preparing to go into hiding. Unable to make him talk, they killed him, and then began torturing Stephen, the only of Phillip's two servants that were present.

"It would have been worse for me," he continued, "if James hadn't returned. The soldiers were watching for him. They knew that Phillip and his household would have been helping the Bishop. James was seen coming from the hills outside Smyrna and so he was followed, all the way back to my master's house."

Polycarp sighed. "And you escaped?"

"There were four soldiers. Three left to send word to their officers. I think they thought I was dead. But I managed to loosen the knots that bound my hands. Eventually I was able to grasp a nearby pitcher. I struck the last soldier on the head, and knocked him unconscious. I used his sword to cut my bonds, and ran here as fast as I could."

"Stephen," said the Captain. "How long before they are here?"

Stephen shook his head as if the news were not good. "They spoke of setting out after dark, but debated over whether to wait until morning. Once they know I have escaped, though..."

Papias spoke up. "They will come at once, knowing you will try to warn us."

"My guess," said Stephen, "is that they will be here within the hour."

There was a grim silence at the news. Polycarp looked at the young man: tears had been forming in the corners of

151

his eyes, and now began to spill out over his bloodied face. "Stephen," said Polycarp. "What happened to James?" But Polycarp was sure he already knew the answer.

The young man began to weep. "He is dead," he said through his tears. "At the last they stabbed him through the heart, just like they did my master."

Strouthion got some linen to clean the boy's wounds. "We must be off, at once," he said. "We have little time."

"Yes," said Polycarp. "All of you must fly, further into the hills. Surely some place can be found. I will delay and misdirect them as well as I can."

The others stared at him in shock. "Master, what are you saying?" said Irenaeus.

Polycarp found it difficult to look into the eyes of his dear friends. "I shall not escape again," he said.

"No!" shouted Irenaeus. "You...you cannot leave us, Master. How shall we endure, without you?"

"Hush: don't speak nonsense, Irenaeus. Have I taught you no better than that? Is not our Lord able to keep and protect the church in such a dark hour? You do not need me; you need only the wisdom and kindness of God."

"But, Master," said Irenaeus, desperation in his voice. Polycarp only shook his head and smiled.

"I am eighty-six years old. Whether I escape tonight or not, how much longer can I expect to live? But all of you must leave, at once, for I would not put you in danger for all the world."

"They...are not in danger, Bishop," said Stephen, to everyone's surprise. "I heard the soldiers talking with their General. They are under strict orders from the proconsul: take Polycarp, but leave the others alone. They want to make an example out of you and hope that will be enough to persuade others to give up Christ. They only took my master because they wanted us to lead them to you."

"That settles it, then," said Strouthion, a grim look in his eyes. "If Polycarp will not leave, we all stay." But Papias left the room quickly, without a word. Polycarp saw him leave and followed.

Words in the Stone

Polycarp found Papias in his room, looking out on the night sky. A single candle was lit on a table and Papias' sword – the one which he had defended Polycarp with many years before – lay beside it. Papias turned as Polycarp entered.

"Well, Polycarp," he said, "You would have given yourself up in Rome all those years ago, and you were angry when I saved you, denying you the martyr's crown." He paused, finding it difficult to speak, and when he did there was a bitter sorrow in his voice. "Now, you refuse to be saved, when there is still time to get you out of here."

Polycarp walked over to where the beautiful sword lay unsheathed. "Yes, I do," he said, as his eyes somewhat absently glanced over the blade. "A man may know, perhaps, when his end draws near, and it is so with me now."

"You are no prophet, Polycarp," said Papias. "Leave your death in God's hands. Our enemies will soon be here."

"Enemies?" said Polycarp. "No, I think not. We have lived as Christians since we were young men. It has been a life of dangers and sorrows. It has been like a war, but Rome is not the enemy. Most of the Caesars have not known what to do with us, and some have left us alone entirely. Rome is tyranny enfleshed and a scourge to men who love freedom, but a greater threat to the church than imperial persecutions has been the plague of false doctrine. These Romans who are coming tonight are merely playing a part, and a necessary part. It may be that from the blood-seed of yet a few more martyrs, the church will become a mighty tree that fills all the earth. Then, perhaps, we shall see heresies vanquished, and peace and truth join hands at last. And maybe the persecutions will cease, one day. It will not be in our lifetime, but perhaps it will be soon." He was silent for a few moments before speaking again. "You cannot save me again, Papias," he said, simply as he ran his hand along the jewelled hilt of the sword.

"Yes, I can, if you will put aside this stubbornness," said Papias, both angry and sad. "And," he added, "maybe – maybe I will, whether you want me to or not."

Then, so swiftly that it surprised both of them, Polycarp picked up the sword and held the blade near his friend's chest. "No, Papias."

Papias was as astonished as he had ever been in his life. "I know you, Polycarp. You might not want me to save your life, but you wouldn't kill me for trying."

"No," said Polycarp, a smile beginning at the corners of his bearded mouth as he lowered the sword, pointing it at Papias' legs. "But I just might cripple you. Provided I don't drop this unwieldy thing in the trying, of course."

Papias laughed a little, despite his growing sorrow.

"Polycarp, the great warrior," the old bishop laughed, "bravely fighting off all his saviours, eh? You know, Papias, this is the first time I've ever held a sword. It's a strange feeling, really. It makes me think of all the old stories of the great heroes." He set the sword back down again.

"There are many kinds of heroes," said Papias, distantly, "and not all are sword-wielders. You are a hero, Polycarp, and I say that your name will live long after the rest of us are forgotten. I only regret the years we lost, and the end that is coming..." He stood, and looked intently at his friend. "But...you are sure? You are certain this is the right road to take?" There was a hint of despair in his voice that he could not conceal.

Polycarp looked at him with compassion and love. He told him then of his dream of three nights before.

"But it is only a dream, strange though it seems to me," said Papias. "Would you base your final choice on a ghostly vision of the night?"

"No, it isn't that alone, Papias. I am as certain of this choice as I have ever been of anything, though I find it difficult to explain why. Remember what I said to Irenaeus:

how much longer could I live, anyway? I would rather die this way – wearing the crown of the martyrs – than to live a few more years and die in my bed, sick and feeble. I still have much of my old strength, and so I can die with my wits about me, and the praise of God on my lips. How He may use my death I cannot now imagine. My only prayer is that the persecution against the church will cease. For that I should willingly die a hundred such deaths."

He sat down in a chair and sighed deeply. "You know, Papias," he said at last, "that I have long wished to die as a martyr. But what you do not know is that I gave up that wish, knowing myself to be unworthy of the crown."

Papias was indeed surprised by this. "I don't understand," he said.

"I am unworthy of the crown of fire," Polycarp said again. "But I am also unworthy of all the grace and mercy God has ever shown me. He chooses broken vessels to show His glory, and He has appointed this road for me."

Papias' eyes were already glistening in his grief, and Polycarp walked over and embraced him. "The last Enemy comes to us all," he said, "but in the grace of God, our enemy becomes an unwilling guide into the eternal country. There we shall go, to rest in joy, while we await the resurrection of the body."

Over Papias' shoulder, Polycarp saw the waxing moon, bright and beautiful in its near fullness. "I could choose no better death," he said softly. Then he turned his eyes to Papias. "And I could choose no better friend."

***

It took the Romans longer to come than Stephen had thought. Three and a half hours passed before torches were seen in the forest. The delay was caused by the fact that the Romans came on horseback, fully armed, as if marching against a deadly enemy. As the torches approached, Irenaeus tried once more to persuade Polycarp to leave, but his only response was, "The will of God be done."

The arrest of Polycarp was fairly uneventful for both

him and his companions. Strouthion, for instance, had been expecting General Julius to be in command of the troops, but found that another officer had taken over.

Strouthion would later learn that proconsul Statius Quadratus had personally removed Julius from command, worried that he would exceed his orders by harming other Christians. The proconsul feared that this might lead to unrest, or even riots, for he knew that many citizens of Smyrna had been won over to the strange Christian sect.

So Polycarp's friends were not in danger at all, and the new Roman general – a soft-spoken, respectful man named Lysias – made it clear that he came for Polycarp alone and no one else would be arrested or harmed.

Polycarp greeted the soldiers, speaking kindly, and seeing that a meal was cooked for them. When the meal was over, Polycarp asked Lysias if he would grant him an hour to pray before they departed. The General, already finding his conscience troubled by the arrest of such a good man, granted the request. They were all in the room – Polycarp, Papias, Strouthion, Irenaeus, Lysias, and his four soldiers – and Polycarp fell to his knees and began praying.

Irenaeus would later report that, "the grace of God filled all our hearts in that troubled moment, and Polycarp continued praying for two full hours. His fellow believers soon joined him, kneeling down, and praying with him silently. He prayed for everyone he could think of: those he had known long ago, as well as newer friends and Christians, and even for the soldiers themselves, by name (for he had made a point of learning their names as soon as they arrived). He prayed for the great and the small, the illustrious and the obscure, and for the whole church throughout the world, and he concluded by praying that the persecution would come to an end. When he had finished, many tears were shed, and even the Roman soldiers were quiet and subdued. At last, General Lysias stood and spoke to us, saying, 'My heart is full of grief and repentance that so much effort has been spent to capture so noble a man, and that I must play a part in such an evil.

As an act of my repentance, I will delay our departure until midday tomorrow, that you may have time to rest and to talk together before we leave.'"

Everyone was grateful for the night's reprieve, and enjoyed a few bittersweet hours together, as well as a much-needed night's rest. But soon, too soon, the morning arrived, and midday came: cold, but he sun was shining brightly. Polycarp spoke words of farewell to Irenaeus and Strouthion, and blessed them. As he turned away from Irenaeus, he pressed something into his hand. Strouthion glimpsed a flash of gold in the sunlight. Then Polycarp turned, last of all, to Papias. "What shall I say?" he said quietly. "Our long years of friendship were God's blessing, and your return a rich gift, all the more wondrous for being unlooked for."

Papias' eyes were filling with tears, but Polycarp's face was peaceful. "I had hoped," said Papias, "that yet a few years, at least, should be left to us, as a recompense for those that were lost. I see that is not to be."

"Papias," said his friend, "these few days have been the best of my life. Do not grieve as those without hope. I go to join Ignatius, and Clement, and John, and Lydia. And our Lord. The fire consumes us, as you once told me, but the flame of the story burns on, ever brighter. One day, the whole earth will be filled with God's glory, and we shall see it together, my friend. Farewell, Papias, defender of the church, pastor of the flock of Christ, friend of friends."

They embraced one last time, and the Romans led Polycarp away. Irenaeus wept, as he looked on his great friend and teacher for the last time.

"No, not for the last time," said Strouthion, as if reading his thoughts. "When Polycarp stands before the proconsul tomorrow, we shall be in the stadium, standing for him, praying for him."

***

Only one other noteworthy thing happened before Polycarp was put in prison. When he arrived in Smyrna, riding on the donkey that General Lysias had provided for him, he was met by the Roman Irenarch, named Herod, and Herod's father, Nicetes, riding in a chariot. They invited him to ride with them to the prison, pretending that they were concerned for his age. Their true desire was to persuade him to renounce Christ. They believed that a recantation by the leader of the Christians would do far more good than a death. But Polycarp consistently and patiently refused, so that Herod grew furious, and kicked him out of the chariot. Polycarp's leg was injured in the fall – a terrible gash that bled profusely. General Lysias bound it and nursed it as well as he could, then set Polycarp back on the donkey, and resumed the journey to prison.

***

It was after dark when they finally arrived, and Polycarp was locked in a cell. Lysias provided Polycarp with an extra coat, but it helped little in the frosty weather, for it had been a much colder winter than people in Smyrna were used to. Polycarp sighed. He enjoyed the cooler weather of the season, as a rule, but to his regret this winter, though plagued by many winter storms, as usual, had seen very little snow.

Polycarp sat alone in the dark, trying to make the best of his situation. He prayed, here and there, but found it difficult to focus his thoughts. His mind began to wander the paths of his past, going back even as far as his childhood. He remembered his parents, who had died when he was only a young man. They were kind and loving, he recalled, and had become Christians when he was still a child. Their teaching and lives had deeply influenced him, though he had briefly contemplated other religions after their deaths. But that was before he met an old fisherman named John.

He remembered the old days of walking through the woods and hills with Papias and John while listening to the stories of Jesus.

He thought of his first journey to Rome with Papias, and their visit to the catacombs.

He remembered the flight from Rome with Papias and Ignatius, and the tragic end to their fight with the soldier by the Tiber River.

He thought of brave little Lydia, and her father Marcus, and the kindness Papias showed by adopting Lydia after Marcus was martyred.

He remembered the visit last year with Anicetus, and he wondered if the church in Rome was safe.

He thought of Strouthion, Irenaeus, and Papias, and he prayed for their safety as well.

He remembered the last time he had been in a place like this, when Seudesbar had imprisoned him instead of Captain Strouthion. How eager Strouthion had been to learn the Scriptures after his conversion!

Just then Polycarp's thoughts were interrupted as a gleam of light fell full on his face. He blinked. What was happening? Then he saw it: the moon had risen and its light was streaming in from a hole in the wall. How had he not noticed it before? It was a perfectly square gap in the wall, as if one of the stones had been knocked out. *As if one of the stones...*

Polycarp turned quickly to his right. The walls were caked with mud, but he began scratching away, scraping off the mud as if his life depended on it. In moments, he had cleared the wall, and when he saw it, he laughed for joy, though there was a taste of tears in his laughter. There, deeply carved on the wall before him, were these words:

"Oh that my words were written! Oh that they were inscribed in a book! Oh that with an iron pen and lead they were engraved in the rock forever! For I know that my Redeemer lives, and at the last he will stand upon the earth. And after my skin has been thus destroyed, yet in my flesh I shall see God, whom I shall see for myself, and my eyes shall behold, and not another.'"

It was the very same cell he had stayed in with Strouthion half a century before. And here, beside him, were the words that had captured the imagination of the new Christian, even as they flooded with hope the heart of the old Christian now. Polycarp bowed his head, thanking God for His word, for Strouthion, for the cold, dark cell, and even for the cruel senator who had built it.

***

Hours later, Polycarp woke up from a fitful sleep and tried to move around a little, his limbs aching terribly. Beside him, where his leg had been, he saw a smear of blood — blood from his injured leg, seeping through the bandages. He stared at the red stain, and it reminded him for a moment of the red roses in his dream, only — only, this red was darker. Immediately this took his mind off the roses, and made him think of his own sins. He felt guilt for the angry words spoken to Marcion. He remembered more words, spoken in anger to Papias, and the resulting gulf between them. But Polycarp knew that these sins were but drops in the great, red ocean of his own iniquities — and still God was allowing his servant the honor of a noble death. But then he remembered the cowardice of Quintus. Would he do the same, faltering before the fire? Or would he find in his heart the valour of Germanicus?

"O Lord," he prayed, "I am not Germanicus, or Papias; I am not a fighter like them. But I am not Quintus either, or at least I don't believe I am. Yet I am so afraid to accept the gift I have wanted for so long. My sins are far redder and darker than this blood on the ground. I am unworthy, and I fear that I will fail you tomorrow." His heart began to beat faster in fear. He closed his eyes, unable to pray further.

Several minutes later, he opened his eyes with a start. Something light and wet and cold had touched his face. He looked up. Through a large hole in the roof — to Polycarp's wonder and joy — snow was falling. Large, white flakes drifted down into the cell. He watched, tears in his eyes, for several minutes, as the snow fell on the floor in front of him, until the smear of red blood was completely covered with pure whiteness. He fell asleep, then, and it was the most peaceful sleep he had ever known in his life.

Fire in the Stadium

Smyrna, Asia Minor, Anno Domini 155

The snow only lasted about an hour, though the morning light revealed several inches on the ground throughout Smyrna. Word had spread quickly of Polycarp's arrest, and by the time of the trial, the stadium was filled to capacity with the curious, wanting to see the leader of the hated Christian sect. Trumpets blasted a heralding note, and Statius Quadratus, proconsul, entered with his attendants and guests. There were many dignitaries, including two Roman senators who happened to be in town, as well as Herod, the Irenarch, and his father, Nicetes, and General Julius, scowling, still angry at having been relieved of command just before the biggest capture of his career. The proconsul and his assembly took their place on the dais, right in front of the spot where Germanicus had fallen only the week before.

Then, quietly, with no fanfare or announcement, Polycarp entered the stadium, led between two soldiers. There was silence for some moments as the crowd got their first look at the man who had troubled Smyrna for so many years. As Polycarp took his first steps into the stadium, he was struck by how quiet it was, but then, softly, clearly, and so suddenly that he could not tell from whence it came, he heard a voice, and he stopped to listen. The voice itself was vaguely familiar to him, and the words were unmistakable: "Be strong, O Polycarp, and show yourself a man."

Polycarp looked around him, uncertain where the voice had come from. His eyes found three faces, grim but proud as he took his terrible walk. It was Irenaeus, Strouthion, and Papias, standing, while all the rest of the crowd was seated – standing in honor of their friend who was passing by. Others in the throng looked at them as if they were mad, but they continued standing. Polycarp smiled weakly, immensely grateful for their unexpected presence, but otherwise did nothing to acknowledge them, fearing the consequences if they should be associated with him in the minds of the people.

He was led forward until he was standing directly in front of the proconsul. Then, Polycarp noticed someone else, standing on the sandy floor of the stadium nearby: a Roman general with a familiar face. It was Lysias, the kindly soldier who had arrested him, and given him a coat. Lysias nodded to Polycarp, and there was a look of admiration on his face. The silence had continued while Polycarp walked forward, but now that he was standing before the judgment seat of Rome, the multitude of people in the stadium all began to shout at once, crying out vile curses on Polycarp, or taunting and jeering at him. Many of those present had also witnessed the courage of Germanicus, which had only increased their hatred of Christians. Now, they were hoping to see Polycarp quake with fear and recant, like Quintus, or, at least, to see him die a horrible death, begging for mercy.

Statius Quadratus let the mob vent its anger for a while, but finally he held up his hands for silence. It took him some time to quieten them down, but at length a restless, impatient silence settled on the stadium. The proconsul looked at Polycarp with a smile on his face, but paused before speaking, like an actor calculating the effect of a beat before beginning his speech. Then, he addressed the old man standing before him.

"Are you the leader of the Christians, whose name has been long known to concerned citizens in Smyrna? Are you Polycarp?"

Polycarp's face was set as he looked at the proconsul, and his voice sounded both ancient and resolute. "I am Polycarp."

"First, thank you for coming today." The crowd laughed and jeered, and Statius acknowledged their response with a wave and a smile. However, he was still wary after his experience with Germanicus, and inwardly hoped for an easy resolution to this trial.

"Let me tell you the choices you have today." He paused and looked on Polycarp with what he intended as an expression of pity, though it didn't quite come off that way. "You have lived a long time, Polycarp. Doubtless you have done good deeds, after the fashion of your beliefs. Have respect to your old age, Polycarp. Renounce your ill-considered affection for the Nazarene – a revolutionary against your Emperor – and return to your home to die in peace. Come, what say you?" The proconsul affected his most radiant, charming smile, and waited for Polycarp's response.

Polycarp looked directly at the Roman governor, pausing only long enough to offer a swift, silent prayer for the man. "You spoke of choices, proconsul," he said. "But thus far you have named only one, and that is a choice that commands me to break faith and become a traitor. This choice I will not take. Have you others to offer?"

The proconsul shook his head like a certain kind of adult does with a child. "Break faith? Betray? Nay, for I call you back to your true loyalty, and to abandon the allegiances that made you a traitor in the first place."

"You call me a traitor?" said Polycarp. "Who is it that I have betrayed?"

"Your country," said Quadratus. "Rome is your fatherland, and Rome is the world. What has blinded your eyes to that?"

"I desire nothing but the good of Rome. And that is why I preach Jesus Christ and Him crucified, for only He can fill all of Rome's lands with beauty and goodness, with truth and light. You ask what has blinded my eyes, and well you might, for I was born blind, as all men are – blinded by the darkness of sin. But my eyes were opened by the hand of Christ, who is Himself the light of the world."

"Rome is the light of the world," answered Statius Quadratus, a little more sharply than he intended. He sighed again, and decided to make another direct demand.

"Come," he said, "let me ease your burden. You seem like a good man. I will lighten your load. All I ask is that you swear by the fortune of Caesar. Say what you will of Christ, or say nothing at all, only swear by the fortune of Caesar. There is no need for you to die today."

"This is but the same choice in winter garb," said Polycarp. "But take away the heavy cloak and behold, the skin of the turncoat. You have said nothing new, so I ask again: what other choices do you offer?"

"That shall be made plain soon enough," said the proconsul. "Yet I feel certain there is middle ground on which we may yet meet. Shall I make your task easier still? Then hear me: those of you who follow the Nazarene are widely named *atheists* among loyal Roman citizens, for you will not worship our gods." Here he allowed another dramatic pause, and he played it perfectly. "You are also known by other names, of course, but..." More laughs from the crowd and another smiling acknowledgement from Statius Quadratus. "Here then is your task and I cannot make it simpler than this. All you must say is, 'Away with the atheists,' and I will set you free.

The crowd hooted and laughed, thinking this a great jest at the expense of the old fool named Polycarp.

Polycarp was silent for a moment, and then a smile began to play at the corners of his mouth. "Proconsul," he said, "I think you have at last named a requirement that I may in good conscience fulfill. I shall do as you ask."

Papias, Strouthion, and Irenaeus looked at each other in some confusion, then watched as Polycarp turned, and with a stern expression on his face, began pointing his finger at the crowd. He turned in a full circle, still pointing at the people in the stands, and then waved his arm at them all, crying out with a loud voice, "Away with the atheists!"

There was a stunned silence in the stands, but only for a moment, and then the crowd began shouting and cursing wildly. One man even leaped into the arena and pulled out a knife, intent on stabbing the vile Christian where he stood, but a surprisingly violent blow from General Lysias rendered him unable to watch the rest of the proceedings, and he was duly carried off to jail to contemplate his folly once he awoke.

***

In the midst of the crowd, Papias, Irenaeus and Strouthion were having a rough time of it. It was obvious that they were not taking part in the cursing and taunting. Several began to demand why they kept so silent. But Papias and his friends stuck to their previously agreed-upon strategy of not answering anyone who spoke to them. Since everyone was trying to hear what was happening down in the arena, the questioners quickly gave up and began to ignore the silent lunatics. "Good," thought Strouthion, as he continued praying for Polycarp, "a fight would not be the thing just now, and Papias looks like he just might enjoy one. So would I, for that matter." He breathed a prayer of repentance and turned his attention back to Polycarp.

***

The proconsul was pacing the dais now, frustration growing in his mind, much as it had when he questioned Germanicus the week before. This was not going well. He had hoped to have an easier time with such an old man, but that was not proving true. Statius Quadratus was, in fact, running out of things to say. The thought of executing this ancient gentleman troubled him greatly, though he would of course never admit that. And he was aware that, the longer he paced without speaking, the weaker and more foolish he appeared to the people, and that was the one thing he could never abide, so he turned back to Polycarp, with no idea what to say, and simply shouted, "Swear by the fortune of Caesar!" As he did so, he brought his fist crashing down on a table, scattering papers everywhere. He took a deep breath, embarrassed by his lack of control, realizing that he was letting the old man get to him. But he could think of nothing to say, so he simply stood there, waiting for a response from Polycarp.

Polycarp decided to turn the tables on the anxious governor by offering *him* a choice. "You are obviously quite insistent on this point, proconsul, but your urgency is in vain. Since you again demand that I swear by the fortune of Caesar, it is plain that you wish to continue to pretend that you do not know who and what I am. Therefore, hear me speak boldly, son of Rome: I am a Christian. And if you would learn the doctrines of Christianity, appoint a day, and you shall hear them."

Statius had apparently been holding his breath and he now exhaled, trying to look imperial but failing badly. He was being backed into a corner, with the threat of death his only remaining weapon, and that seemed so feeble, somehow. He sat down at the table, weary and confused, but Polycarp was still waiting for an answer to his question. The proconsul looked at him and said, "I am not interested in your doctrines. Persuade the people, Polycarp, if you can."

This brought both groans and laughter from the crowd, which gave Statius a small boost of confidence. He stood again, and did his best to regain his composure and dignity, as Polycarp answered him.

"It is both right and proper," said Polycarp, "that I should offer an account of my faith to you, proconsul, for we were taught by Jesus Himself to give all due honor to the powers and authorities which are ordained of God. But as for these people..." He looked around on the crowd with both anger and compassion in his face, for these were his neighbors, and kinsmen. "These," he continued, "among whom I have laboured – feeding their hungry, sheltering their homeless, nursing their sick, befriending their outcasts, giving myself to them for the sake of Christ who showed mercy to me..." He paused, and there was sorrow in his voice when he continued. "These, I grieve to say, have become unworthy to receive any account from me."

The roar of the crowd's disapproval was deafening now, and Lysias began to worry whether he and his men could restrain them in their frenzied hatred of this good man.

***

Irenaeus watched the proceedings with horror, but with a thankfulness for Polycarp's courage. As a budding teacher, he was proud of the grace and skill in Polycarp's words as he answered the governor. He prayed for Polycarp to be steadfast, but he also prayed that the proconsul would show unexpected wisdom and free him. "He is no criminal. There is no justice in these persecutions, and they must end. Polycarp prayed for it; so did Ignatius. Now I shall, too," and he did praying fervently that God would honor Polycarp's loyalty by sparing his life.

***

Statius was now reaching the pinnacle of frustration. He must now deal with Polycarp as the rebel he had shown himself to be. He drove his fist into the table again, and strode defiantly toward the prisoner.

"I have heard," he said with acid anger dripping from his words, "that the Christian atheists are forever calling on men to repent. Well, on that point we find ourselves in agreement. And so I call on *you*, Polycarp, to repent. Repent of this foolish, bloodthirsty religion. Yes, *bloodthirsty* – have I not heard of the secret meetings in which you claim to feed on the flesh and blood of your dead god?[1] A vile, disgraceful faith – cannibals whispering in the dark of their loathsome blood rituals. Repent of this evil, Christian, and come back to the light of Rome. Here, then, is the choice before you: I have wild beasts at hand. To these will I cast you, unless you repent."

"Call them," said Polycarp, "for it is not the custom of Christians to repent of the good, only to return to evil."

"Fool!" shouted Statius at the infuriating man before him. "Your doom is at hand, and your fate rests in my will

[1] A common misconception in Rome about the Lord's Supper

alone. But I," he said, struggling to remain calm, "I shall not be dragged down with you, though you vex me beyond all that mortal man can endure. I return to where I began, and bid you behold the mercy of Rome. You are a scholar and a teacher, it is said: how if you allow yourself a few more years of study and writing before death takes you?"

"How if you cease this pointless discourse and call the wild beasts?" said Polycarp.

Quadratus was pacing so furiously that it was almost a wonder he didn't topple off the dais. "Since you despise the wild beasts," he said, turning back to the prisoner, "I will cause you to be burned alive, unless you repent."

Polycarp paused before speaking, the memory of his dream rushing into his heart. He looked back to Statius Quadratus, and had compassion on the man.

"You have my pity, proconsul," he said at last, "for you threaten me with fire which burns for an hour, and is gone. Yet you are unaware of the fire of the coming judgment, in which the ungodly will be consumed." Now his eyes narrowed, for he sensed that the moment was at hand, and few words remained to be spoken. "But why do you tarry?" he said. "Bring forth what you will."

The time had come, and Statius Quadratus knew it. He composed himself, pushing down the rage he felt at his frustrated attempts to get this old fool to see wisdom. He had condemned many prisoners to death, of course, but only for what he considered real crimes: murder, assault and the like. And though he saw the Emperor's wisdom in desiring a unity of religious belief, he also knew that the Christians were merely law-abiding, hard-working citizens. Why should he have the death of good men and women on his conscience? But it was his responsibility. He knew that Polycarp would die today.

"Polycarp," he said calmly, "this is my final word. Swear by the fortune of Caesar and I will set you at liberty. Swear not, and you will die today. Therefore, reproach Christ."

The crowd, too, sensed that time was running short for the prisoner. The air was still, and even the winter wind seemed to wait for the words that would be spoken by Polycarp, Bishop of Smyrna. In the midst of the crowd of onlookers, Strouthion, Irenaeus and Papias held their breaths, their silent prayers ascending to Heaven, where they were heard and considered.

***

Polycarp fixed his eyes on Statius Quadratus, but his mind's eye saw only the Carpenter from Nazareth: teaching, healing, commanding the wind and sea, speaking to the people in parables, dying for the sins of the world, rising again on the third day.

"Eighty and six years have I served Him," said Polycarp at last, "and He never did me an injury, or proved himself faithless. How then can I blaspheme my King and my Saviour?"

Irenaeus bowed his head and wept. Papias and Strouthion were like grim statues, but the hearts within those statues brimmed over with grief, and courage, and life.

***

Statius sighed, turned to General Julius, and nodded. The General dispatched a herald, who circled the stadium three times on horseback, announcing with a loud voice that Polycarp had confessed himself a Christian. The vast throng of people responded with wild, furious shouting, demanding the death of the traitor. The proconsul then turned to address the people as he rendered his verdict.

"This," he said, stretching forth his hand toward Polycarp, "is the teacher of Asia, the father of the Christians, he who overthrows the gods. This is the man who has taught multitudes not to sacrifice, or worship the gods. What sentence shall such a one receive?"

Then the people cried out that lions should be set loose upon Polycarp. But Philip the Asiarch, one of those seated on the dais with the proconsul, answered that the wild beast shows were ended, and it was unlawful to loose lions at that time. Upon hearing this, the cry was taken up that

Polycarp should be burned alive. Polycarp's dream came back to him again, bringing comfort and courage.

The next quarter of an hour went rapidly by, as the preparation for the execution was swiftly carried out. Wood was brought forth as fuel, and a stake was raised in the centre. When the pyre was prepared, Quadratus directed one of the soldiers to nail Polycarp to the stake, as was the custom, to prevent any attempt by the prisoner to run.

"Leave me as I am," said Polycarp, "for He that gives me strength to endure the fire will also enable me to remain without moving on the pyre."

The soldier looked at the proconsul who nodded his assent to the request. Polycarp was bound to the stake.

"Now is the moment for the condemned Christian to speak his final words," said the proconsul with dramatic conviction. "Polycarp, what have you to say to us?"

But Polycarp had spoken for the last time to Statius Quadratus, or any other man in this world. He turned his eyes to Heaven and prayed, and his voice was loud, yet humble.

"O Lord God Almighty, Father of the beloved and blessed Son Jesus Christ – through whom we have been given knowledge of the God of angels and powers, and every creature, and of all the righteous who live before you – I give you thanks that you have blessed me with this day and hour, and have granted me a place in the number of your martyrs. You have honored me beyond deserving to stand in their noble company. You have made me to drink of the cup of Christ, not in death only, but in the resurrection of eternal life – both of soul and body – through the incorruption imparted by the Holy Spirit."

His eyes descended to the people and somehow found his three friends, again standing in his honor, their hearts breaking, as he continued. "This day was foreordained by You, the ever-truthful God, and you have brought it to fulfilment. Wherefore I praise you for all things. I bless you, I glorify you, O my Father, and the eternal Son, Jesus

Christ, and the Holy Spirit. All glory to you, now and in all the ages to come. Amen."

He bowed his head, and three soldiers stepped forward at once to kindle the fire. It leapt up quickly, and, within moments, engulfed the funeral pyre of Polycarp. He did not cry out, nor did he ever speak or move again. The soldiers who had lit the fire stood by, and seemed troubled, though they did not doubt that the prisoner deserved his fate. But their commander, General Lysias, knew otherwise. He struggled against tears that rose unwilling to his eyes, and inwardly resolved to learn more of this Christ whose followers lived and died so well. But General Julius laughed aloud at the death of Polycarp.

Papias watched, tears streaming down his face, as his dear friend passed from life to death, and into the presence of the Lord God, to whom, it is said, the death of his saints is precious indeed.

***

The flame rose higher, carried by a wind that had suddenly swept in, and it seemed to Papias that it formed a great arch, like the sail of a ship when it is filled with the high winds of the sea. Through the flames Papias saw the body of Polycarp, head still bowed upon his chest. Papias' eyes were swimming with tears so he was never sure of the truth of what he seemed to see – but for a single moment, Polycarp appeared to him, not as flesh and bone, burned and scorched, but as gold and silver glowing in a furnace. And as the wind turned towards him, he smelled such a sweet fragrance – like frankincense, only richer – that he wondered what kind of wood was burning in the fire. The last thing he ever remembered of that day was the golden silhouette of Polycarp, within the flaming pyre. A burning brand, a twist of vine from the pile of wood, caught in the wind and fell upon the martyr like a circlet of fiery gold.

The Golden Chain

Silence filled the room. The story was evidently over, for Irenaeus had stopped speaking some minutes ago, lost now in his own thoughts or memories. Hippolytus looked with a new wonder on his teacher, for he realized, almost as if for the first time, that Irenaeus had lived long and seen much. At last Hippolytus decided to break the silence.

"Is that the end of the story, Master?"

Irenaeus looked up as if he had forgotten where he was for a moment. "The end? Haven't you heard what I have been telling you? What you have heard today is but a single chapter – one of very many – of the ancient story that has been going on for ages, and will never end." But there was a twinkle in his eye as he said it, for he knew what Hippolytus meant. "But the matter was concluded, just as I have told you: Polycarp was taken by Herod, Philip the Trallian being high priest, Statius Quadratus being proconsul, but Jesus Christ being King for ever. But as for Papias, The Captain and I, only a little more needs to be said.

"We left the stadium once it was clear that Polycarp was dead. Other witnesses remained, however, and we heard reports later. Legends began to creep into the folklore of Smyrna."

"Legends?"

"Yes. According to one, the fire could not consume Polycarp's body, and the proconsul, anxious to ensure that he was dead, ordered a soldier to stab him through the heart. When this was done – so it is said by some – a dove flew forth from his body, and such a great quantity of blood that the fire was extinguished. Quite fanciful, don't you think? But because of this legend, it was unclear for some time what had become of his remains. Some said he had not been burned up, and some said otherwise. We requested Polycarp's body immediately, of course, that we might give it a proper Christian burial, but Nicetes, the father of Herod, tried to persuade the proconsul to deny our request, and we heard that he said, "if they keep the least memorial of Polycarp, they shall forsake Him that was crucified, and begin to worship this one."

Hippolytus found this astonishing. "Did he really say that?"

"So it was reported. Ridiculous, of course, but the pagans often misunderstand our faith. At any rate, we found it difficult to secure the remains of our friend and pastor. Some began to say that Statius Quadratus had the body burned a second time, finally succeeding in consuming it."

A sad, faraway look came into his eyes. "But at last, we were allowed to return to the stadium, where we recovered the bones of Polycarp of Smyrna. We buried him, then, and, as you well know, a memorial is held each year, even here in Lyons. You may be interested to learn that Polycarp's prayer was answered. The proconsul, sick at heart to have the death of such a righteous man on his conscience, commanded that the persecutions against Christians in Smyrna be ended. One might say that Polycarp himself ended the persecution, having, as it were, set a seal upon it by his martyrdom. Peace was attained thereby, for a little while. Thus ended the story of Polycarp in this world."

"But not," said Hippolytus, "the story of Irenaeus, Papias, and Strouthion."

"You know the rest of my story, which is still going on, for the moment. But a strange fate awaited Papias and Strouthion. They were destined to quit this world together. You may recall that the Captain was a pirate in his youth. After Polycarp's death, the three of us took to travelling together, engaging in missionary endeavours throughout Asia and Europe. One night, about four years after the martyrdom in Smyrna, we were chased by a pirate craft — a ship captained by the only surviving crew mate from

Strouthion's younger days: his first mate, in fact. To shorten a long narrative, this man had always hated Strouthion, and had vowed to kill him a hundred times over. But he had been away for many years and thought surely Strouthion was dead. Upon his return, and finding the Captain still alive, he laid in wait, and on a quiet night, he found us, with the wind against us, and took up the chase.

"There was no hope of outrunning his lighter craft, so we prepared for battle. Yes, battle. You needn't look so surprised – though it was the first and last time I took up the sword. But we were carrying much-needed supplies to one of our missions that had been devastated by famine. And several families with small children were aboard. The thought of them falling into the hands of those butchers was more than I could bear. So I fought. We won the battle, and even Strouthion – then nearly eighty years old – and Papias, who was ninety, fought admirably well. But they both fell, in the end, pierced with many wounds. It was a bitter farewell, though noble and honorable, and my only regret is that they never heard the end of that story. The first mate, you see, had been captured, and I befriended him – not an easy thing to do, let me say. He had been deeply moved by Strouthion and Papias and their courage in the battle and came to faith in our Lord, before he was executed for his crimes. He was baptized, and became a great witness to the faith of Christ before the end. And so, the work of these mighty men, like that of Polycarp himself, continued after their deaths."

Irenaeus fell silent again, leafing absently through his papers, but soon he stood, and walked somewhat unsteadily over to Hippolytus. "I want to give you something, Hippolytus: something that was given to me, long ago."

"What is it, Master?" said Hippolytus, standing.

"It is a parable," said Irenaeus, "but one you can see and touch." From within his robe he produced a long, golden chain, made of many links. He handed it to Hippolytus.

"This," he said, "was given to me by Polycarp on the night of his arrest. It was given to him by John the Apostle, but John never told Polycarp where he got it. Just as he passed on the golden chain to Polycarp, and Polycarp to me, and I to you, so has the Treasure of the Faith been passed on to each generation. And so it will continue, for thousands of years, perhaps: as long as time shall endure. But it begins again with you, Hippolytus, as you tell others what you have seen and heard."

Hippolytus looked down at the beautiful chain in his hand, too deeply moved to speak. Irenaeus walked over to the window and looked out on the stormy sky. Night was swiftly approaching, and lightning raced and hid among the dark clouds. "The storm will return, and soon, Hippolytus," said the Bishop at last. "We do not know how much time we have, and though God in His mercy grants us much joy, peace, and even moments of delight, we are never safe. But we are in His hands. Every moment is precious, and we are to use those moments to fulfill our callings. Your calling is, like mine, to teach, preach, and write. The time has come for you to put your learning and skills to more practical use. It is time, if you will, to begin forging another link in the golden chain." He turned and looked at Hippolytus again.

Hippolytus searched his master's face before speaking. "What do you mean?"

Irenaeus hesitated, as if what he had to say was difficult. "There is someone I would like you to teach, Hippolytus. He is a new Christian, and steeped in ignorance, but desperate to learn. He is old – not much younger than me, in fact. I asked him to come here, at this very hour. He should be waiting in the parlour, unless I am much mistaken."

"I will do my best, Master."

Irenaeus searched well the face of his young disciple before continuing, and his hesitancy was now evident to Hippolytus, who was growing slightly alarmed. "You have met him before. Hippolytus –"But at that moment, the door opened, and Irenaeus' nephew came in with a man following behind. The man was old, and walked with a bowed back, and halting steps. His hair – what remained of it — was a dark gray, and his skin was more wrinkled than Hippolytus would have thought possible. Across his head and face there was a leather cord that bound a round, black patch to his right eye. Irenaeus nodded to his nephew, who left the room, closing the door behind him.

Hippolytus stepped backward, breathing heavily, his mind reeling, for despite the passing of a quarter of a century, he recognized the man.

"You," he said, "what are you doing here?" But he already knew the answer.

The old man tried to speak, but his lips began trembling, a sob caught in his throat, and tears formed in his eyes. Irenaeus walked over to him, and put a hand on his shoulder.

"Yes," said Irenaeus. "I was sure the passing of time would not erase the memory of this man from your heart, Hippolytus. This is Severus, originally from Smyrna, now a longtime resident of Lyons. It was his father, Quintus, who betrayed Christ only days before Polycarp's martyrdom, driving his young son as far away from faith as one man can drive another. Severus hated the church from that day on, because he hated cowardice above all. And one rainy night, twenty-five years ago, that hatred led him to cast a stone that killed a young believer — your brother."

Hippolytus slid into a chair, too weak to stand. His hands were trembling and his head was pounding. Words eluded him, and his mind was in a whirl.

"But that story, too, has at least one more chapter," continued Irenaeus. "For on that same rainy night, a seed of doubt was planted. Yes, doubt — doubt whether he was right in his assessment of Christians as born cowards. For he saw something in the streets of Lyons that night: he saw Christians, standing with magnificent valour in the face of death, risking themselves for others, and laying down their lives rather than give up their faith. It was only a seed, and by itself was not enough to bring him to Christ. But it was enough to make him miserable for many years afterwards, and it was enough to bring him to my house, late one night several weeks ago, in the hope of learning more about the Lord of these valiant Christians."

Hippolytus' eyes were watery, and he was still unable to look up or speak. Irenaeus paused, only for a few moments, and continued. "He came, not knowing the brother of the man he murdered was here. I only told him that last night. He came, seeking answers, and seeking forgiveness, above all. I have made sure he found it, at least from the One who matters most. But he still needs it from you, Hippolytus. Will you give it to him?"

Tears of bitter regret were streaming down the face of Severus and he looked at Hippolytus as if his whole life hung on the young man's response – and perhaps in some ways it did. But the sheer emotional burden that weighed on the old sinner, soul and body, made him incapable of speech. Irenaeus knew this, and Hippolytus knew it, too.

The Bishop spoke again. "Will you give it to him? Will you – will you teach him?"

Several minutes passed in silence. Thunder rolled across the skies, and lightning flashed again, but the storm was beginning to play out. As the wild downpour transformed into a fine, gentle rain, Hippolytus rose and looked into the eyes of his brother's murderer. He found speech almost impossible, and when words came, they were heavy, as if burdened with the weight of years; yet clear too, as if Hippolytus desperately wanted them spoken.

"Brother Severus," he said through his tears. "Please sit down. I want to tell you a story."

They sat down together, for the first of many times. Irenaeus lay down on his bed, content to listen and not speak for a while. He smiled, closed his eyes, and fell asleep to the sound of the rain.

Behind the Scenes with the Early Church

This section gives background information on several of the key characters in *Crown of Fire*, and talks a little about the process of bringing this story to life in a novel.

Books and Websites
For Further Study

Books: *In the Fullness of Time: A Historian Looks at Christmas, Easter, and the Early Church* (Paul Maier); *The Story of Christianity Volume I: The Early Church to the Dawn of the Reformation* (Justo Gonzalez); Sketches from Church History (S.M. Houghton).

Always check with your parents before visiting any website. Websites: newadvent.org – 11,000 articles on church history.biblegateway.com – A great website for online Bible study.earlychurch.org – Articles on early church fathers, heretics, etc.

A website fearing the writings of Polycarp, Papias, Irenaeus, Clement, Ignatius etc.: ccel.org/fathers2

One: Polycarp, Disciple of the Apostles

"And to the angel of the church in Smyrna write… Do not fear what you are about to suffer…Be faithful unto death, and I will give you the crown of life. He who has an ear, let him hear what the Spirit says to the churches. The one who conquers will not be hurt by the second death.'" Revelation 2:8-11

"Let us then serve Him in fear, and with all reverence, even as He Himself has commanded us, and as the apostles who preached the Gospel unto us, and the prophets who proclaimed beforehand the coming of the Lord." Polycarp of Smyrna

Polycarp was the bishop of Smyrna in Asia Minor in the second century. He lived close to the time of Jesus, having been born less than forty years after Christ's death and resurrection. Little is known about Polycarp's life which makes it interesting if you happen to try to write a story about him. But here's what we do know:

He was a disciple of John the Apostle (one of Jesus' best known disciples, and author of several New Testament books including the Gospel of John, the three epistles that bear his name, and Revelation). Polycarp was also acquainted with some of the other apostles. He had a companion named Papias, who was also a disciple of John. He was the bishop of Smyrna, a city in Asia Minor, and one of the churches to whom John addressed the book of Revelation. Among his own disciples were two named Florinus and Irenaeus. Florinus fell into false doctrine, while Irenaeus remained true to the Christian faith. Irenaeus is one of the key Christian leaders of the second century, and much of our knowledge of Polycarp comes from him. Polycarp was also a friend of Ignatius, bishop of Antioch. On his way to his death in Rome, Ignatius stayed in Smyrna with Polycarp, and later, before reaching Rome, he wrote letters to various churches, including one to Polycarp himself.

Polycarp was also a writer, and his letter to the Philippians has survived to this day. Polycarp's love and knowledge of the

Bible is evident in this letter, for he quotes the Scriptures often.

While in Rome on one occasion, Polycarp met Marcion, the famous heretic, who denied, among other things, that Jesus had come to earth in the flesh. When they met, Marcion said, "Do you know me?" and Polycarp replied, "I do know you: the first-born of Satan.

Polycarp journeyed to Rome while a man named Anicetus served the church as bishop there. The churches in Asia celebrated Easter on a different day than other Christian churches, and some were in favor of forcing the Asians to change their way of observing the day. Polycarp and Anicetus discussed this and other issues on which they disagreed, but though they could not persuade each other, they nevertheless parted in peace, unwilling to quarrel over the matter.

Finally, we have a detailed account of his noble death written by members of his church in Smyrna, which is perhaps the most famous account of martyrdom from the early church. This account chronicles the final words and deeds of Polycarp, and describes how, though he was offered chance after chance to save his own life, he refused to deny Jesus. His valour cost him his life, for he was burned at the stake for defying the Roman governor.

Not much to go by, is it? A lot of guessing is involved when writing about men who lived so long ago. But in this book, you will find all of the known historical facts of Polycarp's life. For the rest, the book was written around other historical events that Polycarp may or may not have been involved in, but which surely affected him in some way. We do not know, for example, that Polycarp was involved in some of the persecutions described in this book, or that he felt about martyrdom the way I have presented here. But we know that Christians were under continual pressure from the Roman Empire and that often meant martyrdom. Believers responded in very different ways to that threat. Some broke under the pressure and denied Christ. Others gave themselves up willingly. Others (like Ignatius in Chapter 10) longed to die as martyrs, and did not want their friends to try to save them. This book explores what it may have been like to live with such dangers, and reminds us that we are called to live valiantly and faithfully for Christ. Polycarp is one of the best examples in history of someone who did just that.

"But Polycarp also was…instructed by apostles, and conversed with many who had seen Christ…I also saw him in my early youth, for he tarried a very long time, and, when a very old man, gloriously and most nobly suffering martyrdom, departed this life, having always taught the things which he had learned from the apostles, and which the church has handed down, and which alone are true. To these things all the Asiatic Churches testify, as do also those men who have succeeded Polycarp down to the present time—a man who was of much greater weight, and a more steadfast witness of truth, than Valentinus, and Marcion, and the rest of the heretics." Irenaeus of Lyons

Two: Papias, "A man of old time."

"...but you are fellow citizens with the saints and members of the household of God, built on the foundation of the apostles and prophets, Christ Jesus himself being the cornerstone, in whom the whole structure, being joined together, grows into a holy temple in the Lord." Ephesians 2:19-21

"If, then, any one who had attended on the elders came, I asked minutely after their sayings—what Andrew or Peter said, or what was said by Philip, or by Thomas, or by James, or by John, or by Matthew, or by any other of the Lord's disciples... For I imagined that what was to be got from books was not so profitable to me as what came from the living and abiding voice." Papias of Hierapolis

"Of Papias' life nothing is known." So reads one historical summary of the writings of Polycarp's friend, Papias. Actually it is not quite true. We do know, through the writings of Irenaeus, that Papias was "an ancient man ["a man of old time"], who was a hearer of John, and a friend of Polycarp." Still, that's not much to go by when you're writing a story and you want it to be as historically accurate as possible. But, as a friend of Polycarp, Papias had to be in the story, so it was necessary that a good deal be "made up." And so we have the Papias of *Crown of Fire*: a former soldier with a poetic mind who, while willing to risk his own life, is not afraid to use his sword to protect others.

Was the real Papias like this? We don't know. The little we do know comes from his writings. Irenaeus tells us that Papias wrote a work in five books; but it has been lost, and only snatches of it have survived: *The Fragments of Papias*. Some of Papias' words from those fragments are included in *Crown of Fire* as dialogue. But Papias was evidently a man who was highly esteemed by the ancient church fathers. Anastasius Sinaita, a later writer, referred to him as "Papias of Hierapolis, the illustrious, a disciple of the apostle who leaned on the bosom of Christ," which means that he was a famous disciple of John. But Irenaeus thought highly of him, and may have known him (as I suggest in *Crown of Fire*).

Though his writings have, for the most part, not survived, his name has; and he is an important link to "the living and abiding voice" of those who walked with Jesus during His life and ministry. And even though we don't know much about his life, everything in *Crown of Fire* springs from Irenaeus' description of him: "a hearer of John, and a friend of Polycarp."

"It is a false rumour which has reached you to the effect that I have translated the books of Josephus and the volumes of the holy men Papias and Polycarp. I have neither the leisure nor the ability to preserve the charm of these masterpieces in another tongue." Jerome (4th Century) in a letter to Lucinius

Three: Ignatius, The Bearer of God

"And in Antioch the disciples were first called Christians." Acts 11:26

"May I enjoy the wild beasts that are prepared for me; and I pray they may be found eager to rush upon me, which also I will entice to devour me speedily, and not deal with me as with some, whom, out of fear, they have not touched. But if they be unwilling to assail me, I will compel them to do so. Pardon me in this: I know what is for my benefit. Now I begin to be a disciple." Ignatius of Antioch

"Legend is what gives history its spice," someone once said. The life of Ignatius sparked one of the most interesting legends in church history, and one that was believed by some of the most ancient church writers. It is the legend that Ignatius of Antioch was the child whom Jesus took up in his arms, as recorded in Mark 9:36-37: "And he took a child and put him in the midst of them, and taking him in his arms, he said to them, 'Whoever receives one such child in my name receives me, and whoever receives me, receives not me but him who sent me'" Most historians now say there is no direct evidence to support the legend, but it is an interesting story. Ignatius liked to call himself Theophorus, which means "bearer of God." It makes you think that the "bearer of God" may have been borne in the arms of God.

But Ignatius' life is interesting enough whether or not the legend is true (in *Crown of Fire*, the legend is mentioned, but even the characters in the story don't know if it is true, and no answer is offered). He was the bishop of Antioch, home of one of the earliest churches (see Acts 11:26). He was most likely a friend or disciple of John the Apostle, and may have known others of the Lord's disciples. One ancient writer stated that Ignatius was ordained by Peter himself. He was known to be brave and faithful, carrying the church of Antioch through many dark days of fear and danger.

He was grieved by the persecutions, and rejoiced when they

came to an end; but it was not his own safety that he prized. He himself desired to bear witness to the truth and grace of Christ by giving up his life as a martyr. Such a desire is strange to those of us who are not accustomed to the terrors that Christians in those days (and in our day in many parts of the world) had to endure. But many Christians shared the desire of Ignatius. To die as a martyr was thought to be a noble, admirable death.

The events leading up to Ignatius' death were much as they are described in *Crown of Fire*. Ignatius came to Polycarp's home in Smyrna, accompanied by ten soldiers (whom he referred to as "leopards" because they acted like beasts). Many Churches sent delegations to visit him there, and to bring him gifts and words of encouragement. From there he wrote a number of letters, which have survived to this day. Later, he would write another letter, this one to Polycarp, in which he said, "Having obtained good proof that thy mind is fixed in God as upon an immoveable rock, I loudly glorify His name that I have been thought worthy to behold thy blameless face...."

After leaving Smyrna, Ignatius continued his journey to Rome, where he was thrown to the wild beasts for the entertainment of the people. Ignatius would not let go of Christ even to save his own life. Like Polycarp and Papias, Ignatius of Antioch is an important link to the days of the Apostles, and a true hero for Christians of all ages.

"I exhort you all, therefore, to yield obedience to the word of righteousness, and to exercise all patience, such as ye have seen set before your eyes, not only in the case of the blessed Ignatius, and Zosimus, and Rufus, but also in others among yourselves, and in Paul himself, and the rest of the apostles. This do in the assurance that all these have not run in vain, but in faith and righteousness, and that they are now in their due place in the presence of the Lord, with whom also they suffered. For they loved not this present world, but Him who died for us, and for our sakes was raised again by God from the dead." Polycarp of Smyrna

Four: Irenaeus, Pastor and Shepherd

"Beloved, although I was very eager to write to you about our common salvation, I found it necessary to write appealing to you to contend for the faith that was once for all delivered to the saints." Jude 1:3

Whatsoever things he had heard from them respecting the Lord, both with regard to His miracles and His teaching, Polycarp having thus received information from the eye-witnesses of the Word of life, would recount them all in harmony with the Scriptures. These things, through God's mercy which was upon me, I then listened to attentively, and treasured them up not on paper, but in my heart; and I am continually, by God's grace, revolving these things accurately in my mind. Irenaeus of Lyons

Crown of Fire explores the idea of a "chain of discipleship," in which every link leads back to Christ Himself. No matter how you first heard of Jesus, whether from your parents, a teacher, a friend, or someone else, that person was told by someone, who was told by someone, and so on, back to our Savior, who continues to teach us all. In this book, we see the first few links in that chain: Jesus taught John, who taught Polycarp, who taught Irenaeus. Irenaeus was the bishop of Lyons in Gaul (modern France). He became bishop when Pothinus, who had been ordained by Polycarp, was slain during the persecutions under Marcus Aurelius described in Chapter One of *Crown of Fire*.

He was both a pastor and a missionary, though his heart was in his work as a pastor. Even his writing is directed toward serving the people of his church. A pastor is a shepherd, and Irenaeus took up his pen to defend the sheep of his flock from false doctrine. Two of his books have survived to this day. In one of them, he seeks to explain the doctrines of the Christian faith to his people. In the other, he defends the faith by attacking Gnosticism, one of the most popular heresies of his day. In both works, he is seeking to preserve the teachings handed down by Christ and the Apostles. He had a high regard for both Polycarp and Papias, and regarded them and their teaching as a key link in the chain, for they had been taught by the Apostles themselves. Irenaeus mentions, in a letter to a man named Florinus, the days when they were both fellow-students under Polycarp. Florinus had fallen under the influence of false teaching, as Irenaeus describes: "These opinions, Florinus, that I may speak in mild terms, are not of sound doctrine...I saw thee in Lower Asia with Polycarp... I can even describe the place where the blessed Polycarp used to sit and discourse—his going out, too, and his coming in—his general mode of life and personal appearance, together with the discourses which he delivered to the people; also how he would speak of his familiar intercourse with John, and with the rest of those who had seen the Lord; and how he would call their words to remembrance...And I can bear witness before God, that if that blessed and apostolical presbyter had heard any such thing, he would have cried out, and stopped his ears, exclaiming as he was wont to do: 'O good God, for what times hast Thou reserved me, that I should endure these things?' And he would have fled from the very spot where, sitting or standing, he had heard such words." It is humorous, perhaps, to picture Polycarp stopping his ears and running from the sound of heresy, but the ancient church fathers were much more willing to fight for truth than many today. Irenaeus, especially in his work *Against Heresies*, is one of the boldest and most capable of these fighters.

"Irenaeus has powerfully and elaborately refuted the opinions of these heretics. And to him we are indebted for a knowledge of their inventions, and have thereby succeeded in proving that these heretics, appropriating these opinions from the Pythagorean philosophy, and from over-spun theories of the astrologers, cast an imputation upon Christ..." Hippolytus (3rd Century)

Five: Marcion, Bishop and Heretic

"But false prophets also arose among the people, just as there will be false teachers among you, who will secretly bring in destructive heresies, even denying the Master who bought them, bringing upon themselves swift destruction." II Peter 2:1

"I will divide your church and cause within her a division, which will last forever." Marcion of Sinope

Marcion was the son of the Bishop of Sinope and was born around 110. He came from a wealthy family, and donated a huge sum of money to the church in Rome when he first came there, perhaps around 140 (the money was returned after Marcion was excommunicated by the church in 144). He taught many things that were rejected by the Christian Church: (see Chapter 11, "The House of Marcion") among them, that the God described as the Creator in the Old Testament was in fact not the one true God, but a lesser being. He also taught that Jesus did not truly become human, taking on a body of flesh and blood, but that he only appeared to have a body. Marcion set up what was essentially a rival church, with his own system of bishops and elders. Marcion rejected all of the Old Testament and much of the New Testament, and so he had his own "Bible" to go along with his own "Church."

At some point during his time in Rome, he met Polycarp. We can only imagine what that conversation was like, which I have tried to do in Chapter 11 of *Crown of Fire*. We know for certain that when the two men met, Marcion said something along the lines of "Do you know me?" or "Will you recognize us?" (that is, Marcion and his followers). Polycarp responded, "Ay, ay, I recognize the first-born of Satan." Whether or not this response was the best way to handle the situation (even if what he said is true) is explored in *Crown of Fire*. Marcion reminds us of the great value of truth and the need to hold fast to the Word of God, that we might not be "carried about by every wind of doctrine" (Ephesians 4:14).

"Marcion...advanced the most daring blasphemy against Him who is proclaimed as God by the law and the prophets, declaring Him to be the author of evils, to take delight in war, to be infirm of purpose, and even to be contrary to Himself...But since this man is the only one who has dared openly to mutilate the Scriptures, and unblushingly above all others to inveigh against God, I purpose specially to refute him, convicting him out of his own writings; and, with the help of God, I shall overthrow him out of those discourses of the Lord and the apostles, which are of authority with him, and of which he makes use." Irenaeus of Lyons

TIME LINE

Some dates are approximate (the writing of *Against Heresies* for example). All dates are Anno Domini, "in the year of our Lord."

33:       Death, resurrection, and ascension of Jesus Christ.

34:       Conversion of Saul of Tarsus (Paul).

42:       Persecution in Palestine under Herod Agrippa.

44:       Martyrdom of James the Greater, Apostle.

64:       Persecution in Rome under Emperor Nero.
          Peter is martyred in either 64 or 67.

69:       Birth of Polycarp.

70:       Destruction of Jerusalem by Titus.

79:       Eruption of Vesuvius and destruction of Pompeii.

88-97:   Clement I serves as Bishop of Rome.

93 or 94: Josephus, Jewish historian, writes *Jewish Antiquities.*

95:       Persecution of Christians under Emperor Domitian .

100:      Death of John the Apostle in Ephesus.

107:      Ignatius of Antioch is martyred in Rome.

109:      Cornelius Tacitus, Roman historian, writes *The Histories.*

112:      Emperor Trajan writes to Pliny the Younger, governor of Bithynia, to instruct him only to punish Christians if publicly denounced. This becomes the accepted way of dealing with Christians among the Caesars of Rome.

117-38:   Persecution of the church under Emperor Hadrian.

144:      Excommunication of Marcion, bishop and heretic.

154:      Polycarp visits Anicetus, Bishop of Rome, to discuss the controversy over the celebration of Easter.

155:	Polycarp martyred in Smyrna.
165:	Justin, defender of Christianity, martyred in Rome.
177:	Persecutions under Emperor Marcus Aurelius. Pothinus, bishop of Lyons is slain in the persecutions.
182-188:	Irenaeus writes *'Against Heresies.'*
202:	Persecution under Emperor Septimius Severus. Irenaeus dies.

William Chad Newsom

William Chad Newsom lives in Liberty, North Carolina with his wife, Angela, his children, Grace and William, and their dog, Nick. He is the author of over thirty published articles, with work appearing in *Children's Ministry Magazine*, *The Charlotte World*, *Agape Press*, *Christian Drama E-Magazine*, and *Sunday Magazine*, among others. *Crown of Fire* is his first book.

CHRISTIAN FOCUS

Staying Faithful - Reaching Out!

Christian Focus Publications publishes books for adults and children under its three main imprints: Christian Focus, Mentor and Christian Heritage. Our books reflect that God's word is reliable and Jesus is the way to know him, and live for ever with him.

Our children's publication list includes a Sunday school curriculum that covers pre-school to early teens; puzzle and activity books. We also publish personal and family devotional titles, biographies and inspirational stories that children will love.

If you are looking for quality Bible teaching for children then we have an excellent range of Bible story and age specific theological books. From pre-school to teenage fiction, we have it covered!

**Find us at our web page:
www.christianfocus.com**